PAPERS IN
RHETORIC AND POETIC

PAPERS

IN

RHETORIC

AND

POETIC

Presented at The University of Iowa

November 12 and 13, 1964

*PN
175
B74*

Edited by Donald C. Bryant

UNIVERSITY OF IOWA PRESS · IOWA CITY

Ψ

FOREWORD

The papers which follow were presented at an invitational conference on rhetoric and poetic at The University of Iowa in November 1964. Arranged by the Department of Speech and Dramatic Art with the cooperation of the Department of English, the conference brought together eight scholars from five universities—from departments of Speech and Drama, English, and Romance Languages—to discuss what seemed to them significant historical, theoretical, and practical problems in the criticism of rhetorical and poetic composition.

The program occupied four three-hour sessions over two days. All sessions attracted considerable local attendance of faculty members, students, and visitors. At each session the papers were followed by extended informal discussion among the eight principal participants and between them and members of the audience. The program in each session was guided by a moderator. It has not seemed feasible to reconstruct for publication the context of discussion which surrounded the papers, nor have the authors undertaken, after the fact, to adapt their papers to the others or to modify them in the light of the discussion. The papers, with the obvious exception of Professor Hornsby's excellent "Recapitulation and Comment," appear here, emended in only minor particulars, as they were prepared in advance of the conference.

The invitations to participants suggested no particular theme or governing questions within the broad areas of rhetoric and poetic as theories of composition and modes of criticism. Each speaker was free to interpret the concepts *rhetoric* and *poetic* as he saw fit, or to skirt them, as two of the speakers did, in favor of historical and textual problems in drama and public address. A prevailing theme, nevertheless, is clearly apparent. In six of the eight papers the principal issue is the relevance of rhetoric, however conceived, in the interpretation and criticism of literature—drama, poetry, satire, prose narrative and the novel, oratory. Questions arising from that problem also dominated the informal discussion at all sessions.

The order in which the papers are arranged for publication tends to reenforce a sense of progression which may not have been altogether evident in the sessions of the conference. Donald Bryant's discussion of the uses which literary scholars seem to make of the concept and label *rhetoric* serves to open the subject with a sort of survey, after which Oscar Brockett's and Edwin Black's theoretical considerations and Bernard Weinberg's and Murray Krieger's demonstrations of analytical method follow in plausible progression. Marvin Herrick's and Richard Murphy's consideration of two special scholarly questions may then appear to advantage as separate but related studies. Finally, Roger Hornsby invokes the ancients to make all whole.

The conference was financed by the Department of Speech and Dramatic Art, and the publication of the papers is supported by funds made available by the Graduate College. Many persons assisted the editor with the planning and conduct of the conference and the publication of the volume. The moderators of the several sessions were Associate Dean Orville A. Hitchcock of the Graduate College, Professors Douglas Ehninger and David Schaal of the Department of Speech and Dramatic Art, and Professor W. R. Irwin of the Department of English. At all stages Professor H. Clay Harshbarger, Chairman of the Department of Speech and Dramatic Art, and Professor Ehninger have been especially helpful. The assistance of Dean Hitchcock and Vice-President Willard L. Boyd, of course, has been material and essential.

D.C.B., March 1965

CONTENTS

U S E S
O F
R H E T O R I C
I N
C R I T I C I S M

Donald C. Bryant

Though the symptoms may appear to be few in this conference, poetic and rhetoric are not altogether at home in each other's houses.
Perhaps they have never been, at least since Aristotle. They have
been associated so long, however, that divorce is probably unthink-
able, though long association may make estrangement inevitable.

I do not propose to survey the historic associations and estrange-
ments of these two complementary approaches to the arts of language. It seems hardly necessary to demonstrate that historically, at
least until the past century and a half, the connection between that
body of theory, principle, precept, and prescription known as *rhetoric* at any given time, and whatever constituted the art of poetry
or of *belles lettres* at that time, has been close. The intimacy in the
Graeco-Roman world, amounting at times to the virtual possession
of poetic by rhetoric, would seem to be uncontested. Nor, it would
seem, need one argue, especially in the presence of Marvin Herrick
and Bernard Weinberg, the 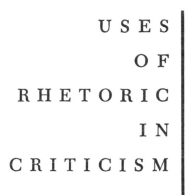 pervasive infusion of rhetorical doctrine
and rhetorical purpose into the theory and practice of literature and
criticism in the Middle Ages and the Renaissance. Thomas Wilson's
Arte of Rhetorique, for example, has much to do with poetizing, especially elegiac poetizing, and Sidney's *Defense* reads like a vindication of a universal art of persuasion.[1]

Of late, however, critical recognition of a social mission in literature has been pretty well abandoned to Marxists, moralists, and the
like. Even so, though most critics have banished *intentional* writing

---

[1] See Donald C. Bryant, "'A Peece of a Logician': The Critical Essayist as
Rhetorician," in *The Rhetorical Idiom*, ed. by Donald C. Bryant (Ithaca, N.Y.:
Cornell University Press, 1958), pp. 293-303.

from citizenship in the republic of literature, they have not necessarily forsaken the term *rhetoric* (mere or otherwise). Though slip-
pery, it is too convenient, and it has too much historical sanction in
literary analysis to be discarded merely because fashion (or critical
sophistication) forbids attention to that business-with-audience which
the term sometimes implies.

I propose to observe what literary scholars nowadays seem to
have in mind when they include *rhetoric* in their vocabulary, and
then to suggest what further use I think critics, or someone dealing
with literature, might profitably make of the rhetorical idiom. I do
not wish to quarrel with usage, but to describe it and perhaps assess
it.

One sort of confusion plagues all users of the term, or at least
plagues their readers. *Rhetoric* is used for both art and artifact, for
a mode of criticism and a genre or quality of literature. Hence one
must often keep track of the meaning in spite of the language, and
that is not always easy.

I. Most commonly *rhetoric* in literary usage signifies formal techniques codified in books called "rhetorics," and rhetorical analysis
means investigation of the use in literary works of the items included
in such codifications. Thus to Umbach the study of rhetoric in
Donne's sermons[2] involves identifying in those sermons the patterns
of structure and the elements of style which are classified and recommended in Keckerman's *Rhetoricae Ecclesiasticae*.[3] Implicit in Umbach's view is the assumption that a theory or an inculcated system
of composition may have some effect on the discourse composed,
especially if like something called *rhetoric* in the Renaissance, the
system of composition is a basic part of standard education. In spite
of its relatively mechanical operation, however, Umbach's formula
does lead us inside Donne's sermons. If it does not reveal very subtle
insights into how the sermon is made, it helps the critic verify his
list of probable constituents, and it may suggest something about
how the sermon came to be put together as it was. Surely half or
more of the orthodox studies of oratory and of poetry consist basically of identification in the specimen of antecedently posited requi-
sites.

---

[2] Herbert H. Umbach, "The Rhetoric of Donne's Sermons," *PMLA*, LII (1937),
354-358.

[3] Bartholomew Keckermann, *Rhetoricae Ecclesiasticae, sive Artis Formandi et
Habendi Conciones Sacre Libri Duo*. The third edition corrected appeared in
1606 in Hanover.

Like Umbach's in method is Myrick's analysis of Sidney's *Defense of Poesie*.[4] Myrick discovers, one recalls, that the *Defense* is a forensic oration constructed according to precepts synthesized from Cicero, Quintilian, and Thomas Wilson. If Sidney later is shown to be more Ramian than Ciceronian, that is because one may easily join Myrick's method to a different rhetorical generator. A study of how Defoe establishes the credibility of the narrator in the *Journal of the Plague Year*, using Aristotle's check list of the sources and devices of ethical proof in oratory, though, perhaps, mechanical and unimaginative, can illumine the *Journal* and can contribute to the history of the modes of composition.

The analysis of poetry also, on the basis of precept as related to practice, or of catalogue as related to contents, is offered as rhetorical—and rightly so of course if the concept of rhetoric is not needed for other uses. The studies of Renaissance imagery by Carolyn Spurgeon, Rosemund Tuve, and Ruth Wallerstein, for example, draw freely upon major sections of Renaissance rhetorics, and Wallerstein's paper on two elegies falls explicitly under the rubric of rhetoric.[5] A. L. Bennett's itemized presentation of "The Principal Rhetorical Conventions in the Renaissance Personal Elegy"[6] furnishes another kind of characteristic example. And just to bring the record quickly up to date, let me mention Sam Meyer's "The Figures of Rhetoric in Spencer's *Colin Clout*,"[7] and Irene H. Chaynes' "Rhetoric as Drama: an Approach to the Romantic Ode,"[8] both published this year. Meyer illumines the poem by detailing its exemplification of current doctrine. Chaynes uses the method less systematically, more for critical convenience. She chooses the terms *rhetoric* and *drama* "to express a relation between language and inner structure" which she thinks characteristic of the Romantic ode. Aristotle's topics for amplification in epideictic rhetoric provide her with several convenient terms for describing certain elements of the ode. This critical tool actually plays little part in her analysis, but she seems to think that *rhetoric* adds enough to her argument to be worthy of a place in her title.

In the foregoing examples there is no denying that *rhetoric* (or at

---

[4] Kenneth O. Myrick, *Sir Philip Sidney as a Literary Craftsman* (Cambridge, Mass.: Harvard University Press, 1935), ch. 2.

[5] "Rhetoric in the English Renaissance: Two Elegies," *English Institute Essays, 1948*, ed. by D. A. Robertson, Jr. (New York: Columbia University Press, 1949), pp. 153-178.

[6] *SP*, LI (1954), 107-126.

[7] *PMLA*, LXXIX (1964), 205-218.

[8] *Ibid.*, 67-79.

least a part of it) is involved. If one wishes, furthermore, one may, for example, attach the label *rhetorical* to Addison's analysis of the ballad of *Chevy Chase* or *Paradise Lost* through the traditional criteria for the epic. After all, Addison does employ the inherited vocabulary of rhetorical treatises: invention, disposition, elocution, exordium, narration, argument, and the like.

To trace theory in practice, formulated and inherited precept in the execution of various sorts and examples of composition and creation, of course, is no tangential or unusual undertaking. It is pursuit of sources, of the genealogy, or perhaps the genetics, of the work of art. It goes on and on, and will go on, often with copious and sometimes with illuminating results. From it comes a kind of confidence that tradition is continuous. It is reassuring to know where a writer got some of the technical or formal components of his work—or whence they could have come to him—and what a writer used of what he had acquired through study or absorption. When the theory, the precepts, the precedents, the prescriptions come from the rhetorics or from the common heritage of rhetorical doctrine, the investigation is obviously rhetorical.

And so one might point to other related rhetorical undertakings in literary scholarship—whether Gladys Willcock[9] or Sister Miriam Joseph[10] on Shakespeare and rhetoric, or Alexander Sackton on *Rhetoric as a Dramatic Language in Ben Jonson*.[11] Sackton, one recalls, finds a source of comedy in Jonson's parodies of the vocabulary and methods of argument and ornamentation which members of his audience were likely to have encountered in their youthful schooling. That is rhetoric. What should we call a study which traced in comedy the parody of the precepts of morality or manners? Still rhetoric, no doubt!

II. A second kind of common practice overturns the ancient hierarchy and makes rhetoric a phase of the theory of poetry. Referring to poetry and oratory in the characteristic idiom of his time, Edmund Burke wrote: "Eloquence in both modes of rhetoric is fundamentally the same."[12] Now the distinguished historian of criticism, on behalf of many literary scholars, reverses the field. In "Rhetoric and Poems:

---

[9] *Shakespeare as a Critic of Language* (London: Shakespeare Association, 1934).
[10] *Shakespeare's Use of the Arts of Language* (New York, 1947). This book has been reprinted, abridged, in paperback, as *Rhetoric in Shakespeare's Time.*
[11] (New York, 1948).
[12] To Arthur Murphy, December 1793. James Prior, *Memoir of the Life and Character of Edmund Burke* (London, 1826), II, 246.

the Example of Pope" he defines rhetoric as "the theory of poems with emphasis on their verbal aspects." In that definition one may be pardoned for detecting the possible defeat of certain useful critical distinctions, even though in the second place Wimsatt concedes so much as to equate rhetoric with the familiar *elocutio*, that part of classical rhetoric, he says, "which deals with verbal devices."[13] Such confinement of rhetoric, of course, is necessary to a parent of the twin fallacies of criticism. As I will imply, however, the *intentional* and the *affective* are not universally fallacious, even in literary criticism.

Related to Wimsatt's, it seems, but less precise and harder to pin down, is R. L. Colie's concept of rhetoric in her brilliant piece on the paradoxes of epistemology in Donne's Anniversary poems. That Miss Colie thinks *rhetoric* central to her argument is explicit in the title of her article, "The Rhetoric of Transcendence."[14] No doubt she means something by it for which an adequate term from the theory of poetry is wanting.

Donne's rhetoric [she writes] reaches out to express . . . supernal unity in, for instance, the lines often quoted as his 'metaphysical' denial of the limi- tations of sense:
> her pure, and eloquent blood
> Spoke in her cheekes, and so distinctly wrought,
> That one might almost say, her body thought.

But this is not simply a stylistic trick performed for its own sake, as the Sophists might have done: Donne is making a metaphysical, a theological, a poetical statement.[15]

And I should add, surely he is. But I wonder what *rhetoric* says in the opening sentence which would not be adequately said by *lan- guage*, or *imagination*, yes or *poetry*. On the other hand, Donne "does not rely," Miss Colie goes on, "as most poets must, on the rhetorical devices of metonomy and synecdoche merely." What gain from calling these figures *rhetorical*, since we are not now investigating the Renais- sance classifications but are analyzing Donne's poetic achievement? Finally, Donne's "devices are rhetorical modes of expressing supernal unity." Why *rhetorical* modes? The term baffles.

But let us not be overnice. Literary analysis is entitled to the tech- nical vocabulary which it chooses. We wish to illumine the composi-

---

[13] W. K. Wimsatt, Jr., "Rhetoric and Poems: The Example of Pope," *English Institute Essays, 1948*, p. 189, included later in *The Verbal Icon*.

[14] *PQ*, XLIII (1964), 145-170.

[15] *Ibid.*, 169.

tion, under whatever vocabulary or rubric. Or don't we? Let rhetoric *be* the theory of poems with emphasis upon their verbal aspects. Let rhetoric *be* the formulated and organized rules and precepts for the making of poems; and let the consideration of poems as they match or fail to match or as they transcend the rules be called rhetorical analysis. But then, what will be left for *poetic?* Horace's *Ars Poetica?* Or perhaps *poetic* will be the *rhetoric* of poems, as rhetoric is the dialectic of the market place, of the public platform. Or perhaps poetic may be the theory of poems with emphasis upon their *nonverbal* aspects. Or is poetic *The Poetics,* and the rest rhetoric?

III. The only actual liability which criticism suffers through such conceptions of rhetoric as the foregoing, as I see it, does not arise from the kinds of analysis which they may facilitate. It comes from repressing, or at least obscuring and confusing, other kinds. Perhaps, of course, a distinctive term is not necessary in order that a critical concept shall be usable, but the precedents of literary dispute suggest that it is. Though the critic chooses to deny concern with the external reference, the social functioning of literary works, still he retains in the vocabulary of his criticism the term which implies, if any term does, the investigation of what goes on between the literary work and readers or audience.

The difficulty may be illustrated in the theory and criticism of satire. It is *almost* impossible to deny that organic to satire is some sort of intentional assault upon the opinions and attitudes of readers, either to modify or to reenforce them. Satire, then, should seem to be an essentially rhetorical genre, closely related to public address. And so it is for James Sutherland. "I take satire," he says, "to be a department of rhetoric. . . . The writer of comedy is content to interest and amuse, and to fashion delightful patterns out of human character and action, the writer of satire is trying to persuade men to admire or despise, . . . to see, or think, or believe whatever seems good to the writer." Swift in the *Modest Proposal,* for example, discovered "just how he was to bring home to the English what their treatment of the Irish really meant."[16]

One would perhaps suppose, therefore, that *Swift's Rhetorical Art* might comprehend the art of selecting and organizing what to say, as well as the art of selecting and managing language. Bringing home to the English just what their treatment of the Irish really meant

---

16 *English Satire* (Cambridge: the University Press, 1958), pp. 5, 15.

[6]

should involve, one would suppose, close gauging of the reading audience in both England and Ireland. Swift, it is safe to say, did gauge that audience closely, chose his arguments, his appeals, his personas, his fictions, as well as his language and his wit, accordingly. That is, Swift had a comprehensive rhetoric of controversy operating through his satires. Of the breadth of the art, Martin Price appears to be aware. He says that he includes in the term *rhetoric* both the "traditional art of persuasion" and "the architecture of communication, its structure and ordonnance."[17] Yet Price's analysis is almost entirely within what seems to be meant by *stylistic*—a roomy apartment of rhetoric, but not coterminous with it. Inevitably, of course, Price considers audience, at least generalized audiences; and in connection with *The Drapier's Letters*, for example, he mentions conditioning external circumstances.[18] Sometimes he even seems guilty of the intentional fallacy. Audience and circumstances, however, he handles as context or background, not as substantive to the criticism. Under the label of rhetoric, therefore, Price's method operates within the texts themselves, and hence keeps the rhetorical art inside the Wimsattic confines.

To a third writer viewing Swift's satire, rhetoric means something still different. Less than Sutherland but more explicitly than Price, Rosenheim recognizes that analysis of satire requires close attention to the times, to the popular topics and responses available, to the potential relations between work and audience. Nevertheless, where to Sutherland satire is a department of rhetoric, to Rosenheim legitimate rhetorical discourse ("ordinary polemic rhetoric") is beyond the "satiric spectrum" on the lower end as comedy is on the other; between lie punitive satire and (below it) persuasive satire. What distinguishes persuasive satire from rhetorical discourse is the ficton.[19] Apparently *The Drapier's Letters*, though they may resemble rhetorical writing, cannot be rhetorical because Swift is not speaking in his own person, even though he is directly addressing audiences whom he may be supposed to wish to influence. Hence we see that though rhetoric as technique, in Wimsatt's sense, may have a place within the art of literature because in that sense it is independent of external reference, rhetoric as quality, or substance, on the other hand, must have

---

[17] Martin Price, *Swift's Rhetorical Art: A Study in Structure and Meaning* ("Yale Studies in English," vol. 123; New Haven: Yale University Press, 1953), Preface.
[18] *Ibid.*, p. 52 *et passim.*
[19] Edward W. Rosenheim, Jr., *Swift and the Satirist's Art* (Chicago: the University of Chicago Press, 1963), esp. pp. 18, 25, 34.

external reference to the world of actuality, in Rosenheim's system, and hence cannot reside in a work of art.[20]

IV. The position taken by Rosenheim that rhetoric, because it deals explicitly with actual people and actual events, cannot fall within the satiric spectrum, is anticipated by Northrop Frye. In the *Anatomy of Criticism*[21] the old terms of rhetoric have disappeared from the critical vocabulary almost completely, and all concern with *docere* or even conscious concern with *delectare* lies somewhere outside the realm of literature. One would think, therefore, that no place would be found for rhetoric in Frye's system. Yet one of his four essays making up the volume, one will recall, is on "Rhetorical Criticism," by which he means generic criticism. Though the poet has no intention to do anything to an audience, to achieve anything with readers, he does intend to produce a poem—some specific kind of verbal structure, normally belonging to some kind of definable genre. Here Frye's argument would show from another point of view in what way the analyses by Umbach and others would be called rhetorical. That is, when the critic clarifies the formal traditions, affinities, and more or less agreed assumptions which bear upon a poem—that is, when he undertakes generic criticism—he touches a kind of *public* element, however generalized or sublimated, which is rhetorical because it represents "conditions established between the poet and his public."[22] This is as far, according to Frye (and perhaps *further*, according to Krieger), as literary critics may go toward examining what goes on between literary work and reader or audience. In fiction, says Frye, "the mimesis of direct address changes to a mimesis of assertive writ-

---

[20] By this time one may be coming to a sense that to the literary critic *rhetoric* is a convenient name for some factors which he knows that he ought to cope with, but for which he has no settled term. It sometimes worries him that *rhetoric* anciently professed, and through the centuries has intermittently professed since, primary concern with discourse as it functions in the world of social action and idea. He finds, however, that even sometimes in the ancient world, and widely in the Renaissance, rhetorical doctrine showed a preoccupation with matters of technique and little explicit interest in relations between the work and the mind, feelings, and actions of an audience. This preoccupation he finds very like his own, and quite legitimately adopts the term without its ancient connotation. Now, among other advantages, he is able to speak of those elements in a literary composition which are there "for rhetorical effect." He is seldom explicit on what that effect is, but it seems to be some sort of spurious effect, different from literary effect, which is produced (presumably upon a reader or audience) when some factor—some ostentation of virtuosity—in the poem or the play attracts the critic's attention to itself.

[21] (Princeton: Princeton University Press, 1957).

[22] *Ibid.*, pp. 246-247.

ing. This in its turn, with the extremes of documentary or didactic prose, becomes actual assertion, and so passes out of literature."[23] In Swift's *Drapier*, I suppose, we still have the *mimesis* of assertion, and therefore literature; in *The Conduct of the Allies* or Burke's *Reflections*, actual assertion and therefore no literature. Where Aristotelian rhetorical criticism would begin, Frye's would end. Literary criticism encompasses only how the poem is made.

I suggest that Frye might be clearer and more effective if he abandoned the concept of rhetoric to mean generic criticism, especially since he uses the term also, and in a much expanded sense, in his codicil on the "Rhetoric of non-Literary Prose." The implication of interaction between work and audience, which always inheres, at least slightly, in the concept of rhetoric, adds a little something to Frye's construction of generic criticism, but it contributes so little that a critic might be excused for reserving it for more distinctive uses.

Use of the concept of rhetoric as explicit recognition of the relations between audience and work is far more significant, it seems to me, for Wayne Booth than for Frye. Booth's focus, to be sure, is sharply on the inner workings of the fiction, but his *Rhetoric of Fiction*[24] is frankly and explicitly a study of the art of communicating with readers, of imposing a fictional world upon readers, of controlling the responses of readers. Booth's justly praised book may or may not add great new illumination to "How the poem is made." I need venture nothing on that point. What interests me especially is that here *rhetoric* is permitted to imply functional techniques and strategies for reaching an audience, not simply for constructing an edifice.

How the poem is made. Surely it is a primary obligation of criticism to develop systems for showing more and more deeply and subtly how the object—poem, play, novel, essay, speech, polemic, television script—is made. Criticism needs to go further, however—or at least *some* criticism, literary or other, needs to go further—to show how literary compositions (at least some literary compositions and verbal discourses which resemble literature) work. The further direction in which I think criticism should go, or should resume going, will occupy the rest of my time in this paper.

V. In one of those careful exhibitions of predigested literary wisdom, a doctoral examination paper in English literature, I found it written

---

[23] *Ibid.*, p. 250.
[24] (Chicago: the University of Chicago Press, 1961).

not long since, "The poem is without description or any scheme or trope for rhetoric's sake—the focus is entirely on Herbert and his relationship to God." Further on in the same paper I found it written that modern criticism has discovered "Donne's nearness to soliloquy or private statement as opposed to the dominantly public or rhetorical statement of the Elizabethans." I would take those words as a base, and I would extend the term *public* beyond what the writer probably had in mind, into what I think that Frye tends to mean by "the world of social action and event, the world of time and process," and (if I may add a word or two) the world of "thought and opinion."

It seems to me axiomatic that much literature, or certainly much of the writing which is the traditional and persistent concern of teachers of English, for example, is a public commodity, and that most literature is such to some extent. That is, it involves purposes, or it acquires functions, which, regardless of the writer's intention, do in fact modify and animate the "world of social action and event, the world of time and process,"[25] which quite explicitly promulgate thought and give direction to motive and opinion. It is creative, and its creativity is instigative as well as constructive. It has to do with the *will* and *judgment* (we in the humanities may still find these antique terms viable, though the psychologists and sociologists may not), and is not concerned with *imagination* alone. Much literary composition not only organizes emotion, it also directs emotion (or if instead of *directs*, one prefers Frye's more pejorative word *manipulates*, it will not make much difference).[26] This is a position, I think, taken yesterday by Mr. Brockett, and it is certainly not outside the critical presumptions of Kenneth Burke, I. A. Richards, and Lionel Trilling, for example.

I would argue, then (and I would hope that the position is commonplace, though I think that it is not)—I would argue that much literature (by almost any operational definition of literature which one is likely to encounter), though first of all, of course, "the hypothetical verbal structure which exists for its own sake,"[27] characteristically encompasses ethical, and political or public events, and the instruments and dynamics which affect those events. Hence, it seems to me that a complete, total criticism which will grapple with all the major literary problems will include rhetorical criticism, not only in

---

[25] Frye, p. 243.
[26] Frye, p. 245.
[27] *Ibid.*

[10]

Wimsatt's and Frye's senses, but in the extended sense implied in Mr. Brockett's title, "Poetry as Instrument." Somebody, I am sure, will be at this sort of criticism, and critics of literature once again had better be the ones.

From the publication of Goldsmith's *Retaliation*, at least, it has been fashionable to lament Edmund Burke's forsaking aesthetics, literature, and criticism for public address. How unfortunate that, "fraught with all learning," he should have sunk to "straining his throat, To persuade Tommy Townshend to lend him a vote"; that born for the republic of letters, he "narrow'd his mind, And to party gave up what was meant for mankind"! Now I would not be in haste to judge what more proper sphere than the House of Commons, the committee room, and the broader political battlefield of public print Omnipotence might have chosen for Edmund Burke. There he is in the company of Swift of the Church pamphlets, the *Conduct of the Allies*, the *Drapier's Letters*, the *Modest Proposal*, and perhaps even of the *Tale of a Tub*, if not *Gulliver*. That same company, of course, is the company of Milton of the *Defenses* and the *Areopagitica*, of the *Federalist* and Lincoln's *Second Inaugural*. This Burke, this Swift, and the others are rhetorical in the ultimate full-blown sense of the term. That is, they *view*, they *address*, they *cope with* publics of which they are quite aware, which obviously they deliberately intend to affect, and which are affected, whether as the writer intends or otherwise. The works involve essential referents outside themselves. The universe of each composition is in direct touch with the constellations beyond. The arguments and the fictions are not insulated from the world of social action and event, but take that world into themselves. Such writings thus are clearly poetical-rhetorical, and criticism must treat them so, not treat them merely as politics whose style may sometimes bear some resemblance to literary prose. A welcome gesture toward a return by literary scholarship to that sort of criticism appears in the recent *Language of Politics in the Age of Wilkes and Burke*, by James T. Boulton, the editor of Burke's *Sublime*.[28]

"Considerable light goes up on human nature," said a critic of public address, "when you contemplate it in its moments of decision."[29] Presenting human nature imaginatively in its moments of decision is

---

[28] (Toronto: University of Toronto Press, 1963). See my review of Boulton in *PQ*, XLIII (1964), 321-323.

[29] Quoted from a lecture by Herbert A. Wichelns in Marie Hochmuth Nichols, *Rhetoric and Criticism* (Baton Rouge: Louisiana State University Press, 1963), p. 10.

traditionally the function of literature, especially of the drama, the epic, the novel. That is, bringing men to life in the imagination of a reader or viewer—incarnating them in their struggles with events, with the motives which impel and constrain and confuse them, and the external circumstances and influences with which they must somehow harmonize their aspirations—these we recognize as characteristic achievements of the dramatist, the poet, the novelist. In the works of the great poets, great dramatists, and great novelists, and from those works, much light goes up on human nature.

In a work of fiction, of course, men live their moments of decision in a universe where circumstances are purged of irrelevancies, where actions are concentrated and heightened. Hence Aristotle considered poetry more philosophical than history. But fiction, though not life, is *like* life; in Aristotle's terms, it has resemblance. It is like life because it is experience in which the audience takes part. It is unlike life because the experience includes equipment for examining the experience, perspective with which to contemplate those moments of decision as they pass.

Men, however, struggle with events in the actual world, in view of the great audience whom they seek to bring into the action. From that action irrelevancies have not been purged by a great designer; the action does not carry with it the equipment for examining it or the perspective with which to contemplate it. Men take direct part in the drama of history, more confusing and corrupt than the stage drama, to be sure, but drama still. They publicly formulate their choices in speech or in writing, and they come to decisions amidst and before and conjointly with their fellows. They bring to life in verbal discourse their embroilment with the motives which impel and constrain and confuse them, and the external possibilities with which somehow they must harmonize their aspirations. And often they exhibit these struggles in discourse where "moral truth and human passion," as Lord Morley said, "are touched with a largeness, sanity, and attractiveness of form,"[30] where in the words of Herbert Read, "some dominant theme has mastery of the mind and orders the expression to the single purpose of the idea,"[31] in short, in something akin to literary art.

Whether from the boards or the hustings, the pulpit or the plat-

---

[30] Thus Morley identified the essence of literature, "Address at the Mansion House," *Pall Mall Gazette*, February 28, 1887, p. 11.

[31] Sir Herbert Read, *English Prose Style* (Boston: Beacon Press, 1961), p. 171.

form, the pen or the press, the monuments of public address, fictional or actual, are more alike than different. They require for critical examination the rhetorical point of view and equipment, as well as the poetic and political.

I would not wish to suggest that all or most literature is somehow within the province of politics because of the kinship of some litera· ture to rhetorical discourse, or that all rhetorical discourse is somehow literature. The widest of qualitative chasms, obviously, separates Plato's dramatization of the trial of Socrates from the record of the speeches in the Army-McCarthy hearings or in the divorce proceedings of Gloria Shapely of Hollywood, even though all these fall clearly · within the province of rhetoric. I would suggest, however, that in certain areas of literature and of politics, areas where literature impinges directly upon social mind and action, as for example in Steinbeck's *Grapes of Wrath*, and where political discourse is animated by creative—not merely decorative—imagination, as in Burke's *Reflections*, literature and the dynamics of politics are closely interrelated. And as a corollary I would suggest that in many areas of political discourse, the man of literary talent, of poetic imagination—the Burke, the Disraeli, the Churchill (to use Stephen Graubard's combination),[32] or the Swift—extends political thought into a dynamic dimension which is not to be derived from the philosopher and the theorist on the one hand or the man of affairs on the other.

Characteristic of this discourse is a live articulation of meaning, to borrow a concept from Frye. It is genuine *fusion* of thought, feeling, and expression, not simply the *manipulation* of thought, feeling, and expression. I am suggesting, therefore, that a radical quality of the best of political discourse is this articulation of emotion, this metaphor. I suggest also that one of the functions of literature, sometimes at least, may be imaginatively to organize idea and emotion (if we wish to follow Frye further) toward political enlightenment or action, and not merely or solely to articulate idea and emotion. Here literature and politics join on their common ground, the rhetorical.

It used to be assumed that Edmund Burke spoke and wrote literature—not always, but often enough when subject and occasion conspired with full mind, strong feeling, and articulate purpose. The passage in his speech *On Conciliation* beginning "The proposition is peace," and his character of the Americans in that same speech, were

---

[32] Stephen Graubard, *Burke, Disraeli, and Churchill: The Politics of Perseverence* (Cambridge, Mass.: Harvard University Press, 1961).

thought to exhibit the essential qualities of prose literature, except for a condition which now might be called a technical detachment from "the world of social action and event." And so, I think, they still do.

Burke's celebrated works, like his lesser ones, of course are not "hypothetical verbal structures which exist for their own sake."[33] They are verbal structures organic to the movement of public affairs; that is, they are rhetorical. But further they are literature and politics, or better, literature-politics acting as one. Whether in the passages which I have mentioned, or in the now more familiar *Reflections on the Revolution in France*, or in the apologia-repartee of the *Letter to a Noble Lord*, the imagination informs the politics and energizes it; the metaphor (as Hazlitt and others have suggested) does not decorate the thought, it incarnates the thought, it creates the idea. This is the realm of Longinus.

The criticism, therefore, which will be adequate to the full examination of a Burke (or a Swift) will be a rhetoric which comprehends essentials of the theory of literature. It will make provision for a mode of composition in public address which is a mode of imaginative enlargement, marked, like Samuel Johnson's, by a "constant and energetic lifting toward generality," and by "the habit of concentrating experience into manageable generalization."[34] A criticism of the common ground of literature and politics, therefore, will reestablish the ancient connection of a rhetoric with a dialectic and a poetic so that there may reappear an art of criticism able to do justice to that socially or politically consequential discourse, whether actual or fictive, "where moral truth and human passion are touched with a certain largeness, sanity, and attractiveness of form."

---

[33] Frye, p. 245.

[34] Walter Jackson Bate, *The Achievement of Samuel Johnson* (New York: "Galaxy Books"; Oxford University Press, 1961), pp. 30, 29.

POETRY
AS
INSTRUMENT

O. G. Brockett

If we understood precisely rhetoric, poetic, and their interrelationships, I suppose there would be little need for a conference such as this. At this moment the one point about the relationship of which I feel certain is that the *criticism* of poetry is a rhetorical venture. It is an essay in rhetoric because by its nature criticism must seek at every turn to gain the reader's acquiescence. I do not have in mind acquiescence merely to judgments about particular works, but also to the basic conceptions of literature which lie behind criticism.

Although we often speak as though a particular critical work is to be accepted or rejected entirely on the basis of its judgments, in actuality there are at least two prior considerations which are partially responsible for those judgments and therefore cannot be excluded in our evaluation of them. [First, are the questions for which answers are being sought legitimate and significant ones, and second, is the evidence which is used to answer the questions sufficient and proper? Every piece of criticism is an implied argument for the validity of the questions raised and of the evidence adduced just as much as it is for the answers reached, and if the reader doubts either the questions or the evidence he usually finds the answers unacceptable.

[Behind these considerations, however, lies a still more fundamental reason for disagreement: basic assumptions about the nature of literature itself.] In one sense there is an infinite number of approaches to criticism, for no two critics' basic assumptions are precisely the same. Nevertheless, it seems to me that it is possible to divide critical approaches into three major types, derived from three attitudes about the nature of poetry itself.

[15]

First, there is criticism which stems from a conception of poetry as expression. Obviously every play has been written by someone; consequently, we may view a work as an expression of the author's attitudes, ideas, and feelings. Furthermore, a play can be thought of as an expression of the values of an age, or of a particular artistic or philosophic movement, or of a socioeconomic viewpoint, or of a particular school of psychology. Into this category, then, are gathered what may appear to be extremely diverse kinds of criticism: biographical, historical, philosophical, sociological, psychological. They are united, however, by a common insistence upon the importance of the *antecedents* of a play to its proper understanding: the belief that literature is to be explained and judged primarily in terms of such factors as the author's personal experiences and unconscious motivations, or by a study of contemporary political, social, economic, or religious concepts.

The second major type of criticism stems from a conception of poetry as object. Here literature is thought to have its existence quite independent of its origins or its effects. Although critics of this school concede that poetry does have antecedents and consequences, they argue that both are outside the play itself and therefore no proper subject of study. Furthermore, it is argued that if these factors are important, they are, or should be, sufficiently indicated within the play itself.

The third approach is based upon a conception of literature as an instrument—for communication, persuasion, entertainment, inspiration, or some other purpose. The emphasis is upon what literature *does* rather than, or in addition to, what it *is.*

The three types which I have suggested are not mutually exclusive. In fact, it is rare to find a piece of criticism that does not borrow something from more than one of them. As a rule, nevertheless, most critics tend to emphasize one of these three approaches.

I would like to reiterate that I have made these divisions in terms of basic assumptions about the nature of literature. It is generally accepted that in pursuing a line of reasoning to its source we can go no further back than first principles. If we cannot agree upon, or accept, the basic assumptions, then fruitful argument is unlikely. Criticism, insofar as it is rational inquiry, cannot escape from the limitations placed upon it by its basic assumptions. As with theologians, each school of critics naturally believes in its own premises. All critics may set out to serve the same god, but they cannot agree upon his

[16]

nature or the best way to serve him. Since the separation into schools is ultimately based upon differences in first principles, it is impossible to *prove* that any school is right or wrong, for first principles are not subject to proof.

The view that I have presented here distresses many persons who prefer to believe in the possibility of assumptions common to all critics. Since agreement appears to be impossible, perhaps we may at least take comfort in the fact that diversity enriches criticism and makes each critic conscious of the necessity of justifying his views. It is in this sense that every piece of criticism becomes a rhetorical venture as the critic seeks to convince his readers that he has asked the right questions, has used the right evidence, and has reached the right conclusions.

I would like to turn now to a consideration of one of these three kinds of criticism, that which stems from a conception of literature as instrument. At the outset, I would like to be frank and state that if I had to commit myself to one of the three critical approaches I have outlined, it would not be to this one but rather to that which conceives of poetry as object. I hope nevertheless that I can be reasonably sympathetic in my presentation.

I have chosen to speak about instrumental criticism for two principal reasons: first, I think that it is in the conception of poetry as an instrument for affecting audiences that poetry and rhetoric most clearly overlap, and second, it is the approach to criticism which commands least esteem today. Perhaps a review of it may help to explain why this is so.

Historically, the conception of poetry as instrument was dominant down to about 1800. Until that time almost all critics assumed that the purpose of literature was to teach and to please, and they judged poetry, at least in part, by its ability to instruct pleasurably. Since Kant, however, the older formulation has fallen into disfavor, and though it has not been abandoned, it now appears in more complex guises.

I suspect that it would be impossible to construct a theory of literature which did not conceive of poetry as an instrument for doing something. Even such popular critical catch-phrases as "A poem should not mean but be," and "A poem should be valued for what it is and not for what it does," cannot be taken at face value. They assume that poetry is an aesthetic object and therefore an instrument for arousing an aesthetic response. The question then is not whether

[17]

poetry is an instrument, but rather what it is an instrument for, or what are the implications of "instrumentalism" for criticism?

T. S. Eliot in *The Use of Poetry and the Use of Criticism* lists some of the uses to which poetry may be put. These include: to commemorate a public occasion, celebrate a festival, decorate a religious rite, amuse a crowd, effect revolutions in sensibility, break up conventional modes of perception and valuation, make us see the world afresh, make us more aware of the deeper, unnamed feelings which form the substratum of our being. This list is by no means exhaustive, but it would be almost impossible to cite all of the uses to which poetry can be and has been put. It is precisely for this reason that the criticism of poetry as instrument becomes difficult. If we are to study something as an instrument, we must first know what it is an instrument for, and if it can be used for any purpose whatsoever, the task becomes overwhelming.

It is necessary first of all, therefore, to distinguish between purpose and use. The *purpose* of a chair, for example, is to provide seating, but it can be *used* to stand on or as a weapon. In literature, I would suggest that [the purpose of a work is inherent in the work itself,] whereas its use is determined by the user and may or may not be the same as its inherent purpose. For example, I can find little in *Hamlet* to suggest that its purpose is to forward the class struggle, but Soviet producers have used it in this way. Obviously nothing short of legislation can prevent such uses, but I hope that we may agree that there is a useful distinction to be made between uses derived from a study of a play and all the other uses to which the play may be put.

It probably should be pointed out in passing, however, that poetry has a special use in criticism. We recognize good literary works in part because of our experience with them. Our ideas of effective structure, characterization, language, and so on are based in part upon knowledge of a wide range of literature. In making judgments, therefore, we tend to [use other works as one kind of yardstick, or as a convenient reference point.] I assume that literary works do not have as one of their intrinsic purposes to be tools for the literary critic. Nevertheless, they are made to serve as such, and undoubtedly most critics would be loath to have this use, which is certainly not justified by intrinsic purpose, ruled out as improper.

Regardless of whether we do distinguish between purpose and use, the first basic question in instrumental criticism is: [What is this

[18]

work designed to do? Or, put another way, what is its purpose? Or put still another way, to what use is it being put? Statements of purpose tend to fall into three categories: (1) emotional or psychological, (2) intellectual or didactic, and (3) aesthetic.

Under the first of these (emotional or psychological) come such statements of purpose as "to arouse pity and fear," "to evoke laughter and ridicule," "to provoke indignation," and others of a similar nature. Also such labels as "a mood of high seriousness," "an atmosphere of gloom," and "uproarious farce" are indirect statements of emotional and psychological responses which a play is thought to induce. Regardless of the particular formulation, few persons would deny that plays do arouse emotional responses. Therefore, the attempt to specify the expected response is not irrelevant, since if a play intends to arouse a particular response, it may be regarded as an instrument for its arousal.

In addition to the emotional or psychological, critics often demand some import which offers "new insights" into human behavior. Generally speaking we are apt to value more those plays which offer intellectual stimulation than we do those that merely arouse an emotional response without this stimulation. Literature may be conceived of as a form of knowledge, and if it is, it must be judged in part by its ability to impart knowledge, either of a conceptual or nonconceptual nature. But how does this idea of purpose differ from the older one which simply required that a play teach? The difference seems to lie primarily in the specificity with which teaching is defined and the manner in which the teaching comes about. Today we resent obvious messages, the sense that we have been delivered a sermon in the guise of a play. We prefer that the "import" of a play inhere in actions and the relationship of characters rather than being superimposed upon them—for meanings to derive from implications rather than explications. Nevertheless, a work is usually more highly valued if it has significant import, even though we may have difficulty in defining discursively precisely what that import is. A major part of modern criticism is taken up with exploring the meanings of literary works. Consequently, I think it is safe to assume that literature can be properly conceived of as an instrument for conveying significant insights.

The third principal statement of purpose is that a play is intended to arouse an aesthetic response. Basically, the aesthetic response may be defined as the perception of beauty. I am not going to pursue the obvious question, what is beauty? but will content myself with saying that the aesthetic response to literature is usually considered to result from qualities in the work, such as internal consistency, self-sufficiency, wholeness, complexity, the efficient adaptation of means to ends, the right relationship of parts to whole, and the total form. It is often said that the aesthetic response is felt only in relation to the "thing in itself"; that is, the aesthetic response is an immediate one which is not referred to any prior ideas of what the work ought to be or do, and that indeed to judge it by reference to anything outside itself is to arrive at moral or utilitarian judgments which have little if anything to do with an aesthetic response. In other words, an aesthetic object should arouse an aesthetic response, and the object should be judged in terms of its ability to do so.

The conception of aesthetic response does not deny the validity of the other two responses already mentioned, the emotional and the intellectual. It seems to me that the aesthetic response precedes and probably contains the other two. By definition the aesthetic response is immediate and intuitive and is felt when we are in direct contact with the aesthetic object. When we seek to analyze the aesthetic response, we are apt to arrive at explanations which are either emotional or intellectual or both. Thus, there is no reason why a play may not be simultaneously an instrument for arousing all three types of response discussed here.

Nevertheless, the aesthetic response is the basic and essential one. I think few persons would deny that an aesthetic response can encompass a moral or other kind of response, or that there may well be responses which are in excess of a purely aesthetic response. It is because of its aesthetic powers that literature is often used for extra-aesthetic purposes, such as persuasion. A play probably will not succeed in persuading, however, unless it is reasonably successful aesthetically as well. We tend to label plays propagandistic or didactic only if the emotional and intellectual purposes have not been adequately assimilated into the aesthetic powers.

Although it is seldom easy to specify with exactness the intention of a literary work, most statements of purpose tend to fall into one or more of the three categories I have discussed. For the moment let us assume that it is possible to arrive at some idea of purpose. The next major question in instrumental criticism then becomes: Does this work accomplish its purpose? In other words, if a play is an instrument for doing a specific thing, we should be able to determine whether in fact it actually does accomplish it.

Answers cannot be sought for these fundamental questions, however, until we know where to search for relevant evidence. Instrumental criticism seeks answers from two sources: in the literary work, and in responses to the literary work. What is required, therefore, is a method by means of which the relevant evidence can be isolated, analyzed, and studied.

It is in connection with relevant evidence and adequate method that instrumental criticism is usually challenged. Before these two problems can be treated, however, we must give some consideration to another basic assumption which underlies instrumental criticism: that a literary work is dependent upon an audience for its completion. Whereas the critic who is concerned with the play as object would argue that everything necessary to the understanding of a play is contained in the play itself, the instrumental critic would amend that statement by adding that everything necessary to the understanding of a play is contained in the play *except* the understanding—that understanding is necessarily something which occurs in the mind of the perceiver. Another way of saying this is: a written work creates potentials which may or may not be actualized through a reading or performance.

Perhaps a simple example might be helpful here. If I write the word *table* on a blackboard, I assume that to most persons it would have a rather specific and agreed-upon meaning, but to a five-year-old child who does not have enough experience with words to associate this configuration of letters with a concrete object, the word will have no meaning at all. The potentiality of meaning is still there, however, and will remain there, and when the child is six the meaning will probably become actualized for him.

A literary work is obviously a much more complex object than a single word. Nevertheless its existence is of the same order. *Physically* it exists as a series of printed words. If I cannot read those words, or if someone does not read them to me, its existence is that of a series of black spots on paper. As sophistication with language, literature, and with life grow, so does the ability to perceive relationships and import.

Because of the ambiguities inherent in the connotative use of language and because of the complex relationship of characters and events in a play, it is doubtful that any two persons ever achieve completely identical actualizations of the same work. How an individual reader

[21]

perceives a play depends upon what he brings to the work as well as upon the work itself, though not to the same degree. The reader brings his personal endowments as they have been enhanced or modified by education and other factors in his environment. There is an analogue here to the situation we find in law when a number of witnesses of the same event cannot agree upon what has happened. Obviously the critic is in a more favorable position than the witness at a trial, for he can in effect re-witness a play several times. Nevertheless, each critic inevitably differs from all others in the degree to which he is sensitive to the various elements of literary form and content. Consequently, what to one will seem significant may not seem so to another.

These variations are apparent in a different way if we consider the criticism written in succeeding ages about the same work. Elements which seem important to the critics of one period may seem less so in another, or may be thought to have quite a different import. In this sense, criticism is analogous to historical writing. The events of history remain unchanged, but this does not obviate the seeming need for history to be rewritten often because each age reinterprets the facts so as to discover their significance in light of current interests.

Such considerations have far-reaching implications about the role of subjectivity in criticism. The internal critic often speaks of his criticism as "objective." Partially he uses this adjective to indicate his concern with the literary work as an object, but he also uses it to indicate his belief in the possibility of objectivity in the scientific sense. The instrumental critic, on the other hand, considers subjectivity to be inevitable. Thus, the response of an audience is an unavoidable part of his concern, since any discussion of a work is automatically a discussion of someone's perception of the work.

There are as many perceptions, of course, as there are audience members, and consequently as many different versions of the same work, although the variations may be slight. Thus, the critic is faced with a choice between an autocratic and a democratic approach. Most critics follow the autocratic method and assume that only the responses of informed and perceptive persons are of consequence. This group's responses are usually assumed by the critic to be identical with his own. In fact, at times a critic may set up such strict requirements for the qualified reader that anyone who disagrees with him is automatically ruled out. In such cases, autocracy easily passes over

[22]

into something hardly distinguishable from egomania.

The democratic approach, on the other hand, assumes that each reader's response is equally valid. As far as I know, only the purveyors of mass culture and thorough-going relativists take this point of view. The democratic approach is apt to make judgment completely irrelevant since all responses are of equal value.

Somewhere between these two approaches is a middle ground. Criticism is by nature primarily autocratic, but even an autocrat can err, and he ought to remain sensitive to the possibility of correction, even from a mass audience. This is not a problem for the instrumental critic alone, but it especially concerns him because of his belief in the subjective nature of response.

When we turn to critical practice, there seem to be at least three approaches to the problem of response. First, the critic may assume that his own perceptions make up the evidence which is to be examined. The resulting criticism is usually called impressionistic. The basic method of the impressionistic critic is to report his own responses and then attempt to analyze, explain, or recreate them for his readers. Such extreme subjectivism is, by current standards, pure muddle-headedness, and it is easily dismissed when it takes the form of such statements as A. E. Housman's that he could tell a good poem by the sensation in the pit of his stomach. Impressionistic criticism at its best is not so naive, even though the results are not entirely defensible. Nevertheless, we should remember that it is based on a conviction that the method being used is the correct one. Anatole France was probably sincere when he wrote: "To be frank, the critic ought to say: 'Gentlemen, I am going to speak about myself apropos of Shakespeare, apropos of Racine.'" As a result of such an attitude we have a great deal of criticism written near the end of the nineteenth century which purported to describe "the soul journeying among masterpieces." The product, from our point of view, was something like a Cook's tour of the great works, and though the tour was often conducted by a sensitive guide, as in any quick tour, what was revealed is often found to be superficial on closer examination. Although impressionistic criticism reached its peak during the nineteenth century, it is always with us.

A second approach is often discussed as a possibility but seldom practiced because an adequate method for employing it is still lacking. Here the emphasis is upon the response of persons other than the critic—the reading public, the theatre-going public, or some portion of them. Subjective responses are still the principal object of study, but the problem now is: How can the subjective responses of an audience be studied objectively? So far we have not progressed beyond rather gross measurements of response through the use of machines, questionnaires, television ratings, and devices of a similar nature. This is not to say that some of these gross measurements have not been helpful in supplementing information gained in other ways. I have little doubt that sophistication in measuring response will grow and that it may be possible at some time in the future to gather reasonably specific information about audience response, which can be related to factors internal to the work.

The third approach to the problem of response is that usually found in internal criticism. Here response is thought to be inherent in the written work. It is deduced from an analysis of the structure, the relationship of characters, the implied and expressed meanings, the mood, and similar factors. While the impressionistic critic tends to assume that *his response somehow contains the work,* the internal critic tends to see *the response as contained in the work.* The internal critic usually assumes that the response of an audience is irrelevant, since analysis implies all that needs to be said about response. Furthermore, it is argued that unless the desired response is sufficiently clear from the play, we would not be able to read it satisfactorily—the fact that we can make sense of the work is evidence that it has at least partially embodied the response. Obviously, here the subjective element has been reduced as far as it can be, though to the instrumentalist it is still there in the perception of the critic who is making the analysis.

Of these three basic approaches, one is completely subjective, one seeks to study subjective responses objectively, and one attempts to be completely objective. It should be clear, however, that these three approaches can be combined. That is, there is no reason why the critic who begins with his impressions cannot go back to the literary work to find the explanations which account for his response. Nor is there any reason why having done so he might not attempt to check what he has discovered against the testimony of others on the same subject. The more emphasis placed upon elements in the literary work, however, the more instrumental criticism resembles internal criticism.

What I have tried to convey in this paper is that instrumental criticism, like all other kinds, begins with certain basic assumptions about the nature of poetry itself. Here the assumption is that poetry is intended to do something to an audience. Because of this basic premise,

[24]

instrumental criticism must ask certain questions and ignore others. The basic questions are: What does the work intend to do? To what extent is it successful in accomplishing its intentions? To answer the questions, relevant evidence is sought from two sources: the work, and responses to the work. Although we have reasonably satisfactory methods of analyzing a literary work, we have not developed sufficiently refined methods of objectifying and analyzing responses to the work. Thus, that portion of instrumental criticism which is based upon analysis of the literary work does not differ markedly from internal criticism, while that which is based upon audience response is often of doubtful validity because the evidence cannot be examined adequately. The judgments reached, therefore, are open to question insofar as they are dependent upon evidence attributed to audience response.

Ultimately, it seems to me, instrumental criticism does ask questions which should be asked, even though the answers it can supply are not entirely satisfactory. Until its judgments are more trustworthy, however, instrumental criticism will probably continue to be primarily supplementary to other critical approaches.

FRAME OF REFERENCE IN RHETORIC AND FICTION

Edwin Black

We would probably all agree that the relationship between rhetoric and poetic has gone too long unilluminated, at least in any systematic way. We have faith that there is some difference between the two, and we are accustomed to consigning discourses to one or the other, but it is becoming increasingly difficult to disguise the theoretical dishevelment which we find at the boundary between rhetoric and poetic. Confronting the discourse whose force must be accounted for by a minute analysis of its texture rather than the gross examination of its structure, too many rhetorical critics are inclined to call it "poetry," and leave the hard work to their colleagues in literature. And baffled by the discourse that is unfashionable in the prevailing literary climate, or that sustains a sentimental or naive attitude toward language itself, or the discourse whose substance is too fragile for the pretensions of its form, too many critics are disposed to dismiss it as "mere rhetoric," and leave the dirty work of biopsy to those with less tender gag reflexes.

It is, I take it, a growing sense that our theories must better comport with the untidy facts of linguistic behavior that has recommended a conference of this sort. And it is in and because of this ambiance that I regard this as the occasion for an exploration. I beg your leave to approach my subject in an exploratory spirit, submitting, not a collection of settled conclusions, but rather some tentative and perhaps tendentious hypotheses. As you might expect, I shall consider my subject, Frame of Reference in Rhetoric and Fiction, with the bias of a rhetorician, and I shall therefore begin by giving you some idea of my view of rhetoric. It is a view which I try to expound at some length elsewhere,* and which I can only sketch here.

Imagine, if you will, a scale whereon rhetorical discourses are arranged according to the intensity of conviction that each was capable of promoting in auditors. We would find, at one end of the scale, a form of didacticism promoting a disinterested, transitory, tentative approbation. This genre of discourse would consist of the mildest kinds of statements you can imagine which might still be considered to have persuasive intent: perhaps unelaborated statements of preference, or reluctant advice-giving, or something like that. At the other end of the scale we would find a form of suasion promoting radical, permanent, extensive alterations in belief. I suppose we might find brainwashing at the furthest point on that end of the scale, but if you wanted a genre that depended more on purely linguistic techniques, it might consist of revivalistic sermons or of some of the impassioned political discourses that we are inclined to call demogoguery.

Between these two extremes we would find every other sort of rhetorical discourse, placed on the scale according to its latent power to affect human beings. We would have, then, a scale of rhetorical discourses graded according to their potential effects. But remember, we have judged the potential effects of the discourses by the characteristics of the discourses themselves. Our criterion of judgment is the potential effect of the discourse, but the raw material of judgment is the discourse's character, so that, although the principle of our scale —potential effect—may seem to be something outside the discourse, something it may *do*, we have determined what the discourse may do by observing nothing except what it *is*. Therefore, we would be constructing our scale according to the inherent characteristics of the discourses and not anything external to them.

Now, there is no theoretical limit to the refinement we could give our scale. We could, if we wanted, construct a scale in which each individual discourse was distinguished from every other, because it seems safe to assume that no two discourses can have identical effects on an audience. However, I think you would agree that that would be an awfully tedious labor, and frustrating too, because we would find the discourses accumulating faster than we could place them, and so we would be constantly falling behind. That is why my scale of *all* rhetorical discourses is a theoretical model, only.

The fact is that if we really began distributing rhetorical discourses

---

* Mr. Black's *Rhetorical Criticism: a Study in Method* (New York: Macmillan, 1965) was still in press when this paper was presented.—*Ed.*

along a scale of the sort I have suggested, we would probably find congregations of them forming at various points. We would, in sum, tend to group bunches of them together. This is because, first, owing to the existence in our culture, and probably in every other culture as well, of relatively stable rhetorical conventions, we would find groups of discourses that went about their business in much the same way; and second, because our language (I am talking about English), rich and exact as it can be, is weak in its capacity for conveying subtle differences in psychological states, in other words, in audience effects. We would be tempted, then, to group discourses along our scale into genres.

The literary critic is accustomed to this sort of grouping. He has the term "lyric poetry" to refer to a certain group of discourses which share a certain range of potential effects, and another term, "dramatic poetry," to refer to another group with a different range of potential effects. We know perfectly well that he is able to distinguish one lyric poem from another, but he often finds it enlightening to consider poems taxonomically instead of individually, and so he is disposed to group them into genres. He is especially disposed to do this when he wants to make general statements about poetry instead of an appraisal of a single poem. He may even find it impossible to appraise a single poem unless he is equipped with some general statements about poetry.

So far, then, we have not encountered any procedures that are in themselves unusual, even if their application to rhetoric has not been abundant. Let us focus, for a beginning, on a point on the scale where we may expect to find the most familiar of rhetorical discourses, and then go from there to less familiar points.

Somewhere near the midpoint in our scale we would probably find accumulating a group of discourses to which we may give the name "argumentation." We would be prone to give them this name not just because these discourses seemed to assume an answering opposition—most, and perhaps even all rhetorical discourses do that—but because they depended on logical or pseudo-logical arguments for their persuasiveness, and because they were reasonable, if not indeed rational, in tone.

If we were to examine these argumentative discourses carefully in an effort to determine how they work, and if we were to exclude from our examination all other rhetorical discourses, we might well end by saying, "The enthymeme is the very body and substance of persuasion." If we said that, we would not only be accurate concerning argumentative discourse, we would also be plagiarists because, as you have recognized, the statement is from Aristotle's *Rhetoric,* and it was, I hold, the genre of argumentation that he was almost exclusively concerned with.

As you know, an enthymeme is a syllogism whose major premise is a popular belief. Thus, if we heard a politician angrily argue that the X Bill is a fascist measure, we could surmise that he assumed his audience to be opposed to fascist measures, and that he was leaving it to his audience to infer that the X Bill is to be opposed. The politician would be using an enthymeme. To call a discourse "enthymematic," then, is to suggest that it trades upon a body of settled convictions, attitudes and values. I should like to suggest the term "frame of reference" to refer to this body of convictions, attitudes, and values. This would leave me saying that enthymematic procedures trade upon the audience's frame of reference.

Just about everyone we know has a frame of reference—one that is likely to remain stable and intact throughout his adult life. It is true that he will encounter rhetors who try to make changes in his frame of reference—changes, that is, in the convictions by which he assesses other convictions—but even when the rhetor is successful, the changes he is able to make are usually peripheral. It is common for us to change this or that element in our frame of reference, but it is uncommon for us to change the whole character of our frame of reference.

Now I ask you, without even the grace of a transition, to project yourself into a totally different situation from the one that you now occupy. Imagine that, through a series of appalling disasters, your whole society has come undone. Imagine that its chief institutions, of government, of education, of economics, have ceased to function. The standard courtesies have been replaced by brutish grasping. The normal cues for feeling have gone wild, so that tragic events provoke some to laughter, and comedy drives others to tears. Your painfully earned prestige will command nothing but scorn; your learning solicits derision; your manners merit mockery; your loyalties are rewarded with contempt, and your affections with indifference. And in this chaos, as in a Hobbesian nightmare, every man is turned back within himself, and every other man becomes his rival and his enemy.

That frame of reference of which I have spoken is now severely undermined. You discover, for the first time, the extent to which your deepest convictions depend upon the validity of your expectations, and now that you are deprived of legitimate expectations, the confident beliefs that were superimposed upon them have become barren shadows. There may be no manifestation of this inner bankruptcy. You may go on clinging to the forms of your old convictions, lamely conserving them, reciting them even, as if they were a litany; but this hollow perseveration would only be for lack of an alternative—a feeble hold on sanity while you wait for someone to determine your destiny for you.

You have, of course, recognized the condition that I am describing. It is but one form of what goes by the name "alienation"—a term that has, I am sorry to say, become a literary cliché. But trite as the term is, I must use it, because it points to a reality, a condition that, because of its occurence repeatedly in modern European history, we must postulate as at least a potentiality for any contemporaneous mass audience that we care to examine. And if we asked what sort of rhetorical discourse we might expect to occur in the condition that I have described, we would find our focus shifting from argumentation toward that end of the scale that has brainwashing as its terminus.

There would be no possibility of enthymematic procedures with this sort of traumatized audience. The frame of reference has disintegrated; its marrow has seeped away, so that it is disassociated from motives. The arguer, who proceeds by making his themes consonant with his auditors' convictions, no longer addresses this audience, because what is left of its convictions is too pathetically little to respond to consonant themes. The pre-eminent facts about this audience are, first, that its beliefs are no longer viable, and second, that, as a result of lacking firm beliefs, its emotions are unfocussed and consist of a disoriented anxiety.

Now if, as reasoning animals, we seek to make our beliefs consistent with one another, and this quest provides the motive force for enthymematic argument, is there anything with which we seek to make our *feelings* consistent? The answer, I think, is obvious. We seek, always, to make our feelings consistent with reality. We point to objective dangers to justify our fears, to objective inequities to justify our anger, to objective reversals to justify our depressions, to objective misdeeds to justify our remorse. If one of us begins feeling emotions that are unattached to an objective reality, his emotional system is diagnosed as malfunctioning, and he is treated for the illness. Thus it is that rhetorical discourse addressed to the traumatized and alienated audience—a condition, by the way, that rhetorical discourse itself may well have promoted—that discourse does not proceed argumentatively. Rather, its traffic is in realities. It does not argue; it describes. The discourse presents a view of the world that will be consonant with the emotional state of the audience, and that view of the world is accepted by the auditors as their new frame of reference because they need it to sanction what they already feel. I shall call this genre of rhetorical discourse "exhortation," and note that the consequences of the exhortative discourse may not be simply the inculcation of a new belief in the auditor, but the radical conversion of the auditor to a whole new frame of reference.

We do not find exhortative discourses relying on arguments for their persuasiveness because, of course, they are establishing the conditions in which argument itself is possible. Rather, these discourses rely primarily on *style*. First of all, they share in common—at least, those that I have examined—extensive passages of concrete description; not arguments and their accompanying support. One is brought by them vividly to see the torments that the sinner will suffer in hell, or the concrete injustices promulgated by the tyrannical government. And second, because this sort of discourse is concerned more with realities than with arguments, it will extensively substitute the verb "is" for "should"; it will make factual assertions where the argumentative discourse would make moral claims.

We have, then, two genres of rhetorical discourse: argumentation, which relies on the structure of discourse (arguments), and which is efficacious only where presuppositions are shared in common by members of an audience; and exhortation, which relies on the texture of discourse (style), and which is efficacious when only language is common to an audience, but not necessarily when presuppositions are. Argumentation works *from* the audience's frame of reference, building upon it a superstructure of commitments, or perhaps inducing relatively minor modifications in the frame of reference. Exhortation works directly *on* the frame of reference, either promoting drastic alterations in its character or, where it has been severely weakened, substituting a new frame of reference for the old one.

Before I go on spinning my web, I had better say something more about this concept, "frame of reference." I formerly referred to it as a settled body of convictions, attitudes, and values, and as the convictions by which one assesses other convictions. These excessively succinct characterizations might lead you to conclude that a frame

[31]

of reference is merely a collection of firmly held beliefs, and that a critic might have successfully described an audience's frame of reference if he has made a list of their strongest opinions. Such a view would not correspond to my meaning. I have toyed with the notion of simply using the phrase "moral values" instead of "frame of reference," on the grounds that everyone understands what a "moral value" is, but I was discouraged when I took an informal poll and failed to find anyone who could define the term clearly. I decided then that I would have to risk imposing on my audience by trotting out a less familiar phrase, and that phrase is "frame of reference."

You may understand a person's frame of reference to refer to his moral values *provided* you conceive of moral values as ways in which men perceive and understand their experiences; but I must warn you that that is not a common way of conceiving of moral values. A frame of reference would be that conceptual order which, manifested in behavior, we call morality, and when evidenced in understanding, we call perception.

Christian messianism has been a frame of reference for millions of people. Marxism too has been one. In both cases, the true believer comes to experience and to appraise events in terms of his frame of reference. It is less a congeries of beliefs than an instrument of belief. It is the rock bottom of one's consciousness, the foundation of one's impersonal perspective. A person's frame of reference is not something he opines; it is something he is deeply convinced of, and it is through it that he determines what he believes and how he shall believe it.

Thus far I have hypothesized two modes of persuasion: enthymematic, which elaborates the implications of a stable frame of reference; and exhortative, which substantially alters the frame of reference itself. I now carry my argument a step further by hypothesizing two parallel modes of literature: enthymematic—or we might call it "mimetic" in the narrowest sense—based upon the frame of reference shared by a body of readers; and another literature, which I shall not name just yet, which addresses itself directly to the inculcation of a frame of reference. I suggest that the types are parallel in two respects: First, the rhetorical type and its corresponding literary type have in common similar strategies. And second, the rhetorical type and its corresponding literary type have in common potentially similar effects on their auditors.

Now, I doubt that you have ever heard the term "enthymematic" applied to works of fiction; I am sure that I have not. And because it suggests an unusual grouping of literary works, we would probably find within the enthymematic genre works that we are accustomed to distinguishing from one another, and we may also find works that conventionally we group together now being pulled apart, some to be considered enthymematic and some not. However, there is at least one conventional genre of literature that, I suspect, would fall entirely within the enthymematic class, and it might be useful if we considered it briefly as a paradigm. That conventional genre is comedy. I am suggesting, then, that comedic fiction resembles argumentative discourse in that both take for granted and exploit the audience's frame of reference, but neither can promote extensive changes in that frame of reference.

Laughter, which is the characteristic response to a comedic effect, seems to be a physiological mystery. Insofar as I am able to determine by consulting with some people who are supposed to know about these things, sometimes laughter seems to be controlled by the central nervous system, at other times it seems to be controlled by the autonomic nervous system. It is a puzzling kind of behavior. And where the expert is baffled, the layman may presume to speculate.

Apparently, the word "laughter," is, like the word "madness," a gross and imprecise term referring to behaviors that are widely variant in their causes. Some laughter is volitional; that is, we may control the impulse to laugh. But sometimes we are quite helpless to control the impulse; it is a physiological impossibility. Obviously, the laughter that we grant a comedic effect is volitional; no one is tickling the bottom of our feet. Obviously also, there are individual and societal variations in the comedic effects that will provoke laughter, and these variations will not depend simply on whether one understands the effect to be an attempt at comedy, but more essentially on whether one thinks the effect to be comical.

Let us consider only one aspect of laughter: laughter as a comment; laughter as a statement. If you will consider those occasions when you have laughed in order to communicate something, you may find plausible my suggestion that sometimes laughter is the expression of a moral judgment. This view, of course, is not original. It is a view common to both Freud and Bergson, although each of them so takes it for granted, and is so preoccupied with the object that will evoke this moral judgment, that the view has not, I think, been sufficiently noted. What may be more exotic is my suggestion that this laughter of moral judgment is the principal behavioral effect of comedy.

[33]

Comedy proceeds by promoting in its auditors a series of moral judgments. These judgments are, I believe, invariably adverse, but they are also mild. They are judgments that a tort, not a crime, has been committed. And if it is the case that comedy promotes the laughter of moral judgment, then it would follow that comedy is enthymematic, because a judgment is—as Aristotle suggested—the result of an enthymeme, being the inference yielded by the application of a general conviction to a specific case.

Mind you, I have only suggested that the laughter of moral judgment is the *principal* behavioral effect of comedy, not its only effect. We must grant the possibility that a given comedy may provide cues to other kinds of laughter as well, and perhaps these other kinds of laughter are more easily evoked by the comedy because of their proximity to the cues to moral laughter. It would be interesting to inquire whether there is any correlation between the kind of cues that a comedy provides and the general aesthetic quality of the comedy; in other words, whether a comedy which was exclusively enthymematic would be of a higher quality than one that mixed enthymemes with other sorts of provocations. Such an inquiry would require much more information about the varieties of laughter than we now have. But for the present, at least, I must content myself with the suggestion that comedy is enthymematic, that it trades upon a fairly stable frame of reference which it assumes in its audience, and that this characteristic—though it may be true of other kinds of literature—is certainly not true of all literature. The extent to which pathos is enthymematic, for example, is exactly the extent to which it is sentimental, and thus fails as pathos.

There remains one other hypothesis: That there is a literature corresponding to the rhetorical genre of exhortation—one which addresses itself directly to the inculcation in the reader of a frame of reference. Probably you have already anticipated what literature that is. It is a type that cuts across generic lines, but yet that may itself be considered a genre. It is what might best be called mythic literature, by which I mean those works that create and populate a whole world—a world with its own moral economy, its own rules of decorum, its own cues for feeling. It is a world alien to the one that we, the auditors, inhabit, but one that we can clearly recognize as an alternative. It is the world of Dostoevski's underground, or Mark Twain's raft on the Mississippi, or Sophocles' Thebes.

There are differences, of course, between mythic literature and its rhetorical counterpart. One does not require an emotional trauma to confront the world of fiction. We are disposed to confront it on its own terms by a conventional response that we are prepared to grant: "that willing suspension of disbelief for the moment that constitutes poetic faith." We are initially prepared to surrender ourselves to the claims of a work of fiction, to open ourselves to the author's manipulation. Indeed, the act of reading a novel or even sitting in a crowded theatre witnessing a serious play is a decidedly solitary act, so that even the rhetorical auditor's state of alienation is duplicated in a benign form—a form that does not seem threatening to the auditor of fiction because he knows it to be temporary and he can terminate it at will. We have, then, a parallel between the state of susceptibility to radical conversion and the "act of poetic faith," the latter being an innocent and governable rehearsal of the former. I would further suggest that whatever true we are able to say of one may also very well be true of the other. What literary critics have told us about mythic literature says much about exhortative discourse, and, from the point of view of rhetoric, I do not think it a mere piety but rather the exact truth to observe that one who has surrendered himself to a masterwork of mythic fiction has become thereby a different man, for the work has quite literally persuaded him.

What I have tried to do in these few pages is to suggest how the typological approach common to literary criticism may illuminate rhetoric, and how rhetoric's angle of vision may sometimes illuminate literature. What is the difference between the two? What, really, is the difference between the squalid world of the John Birch Society and the world of Shakespeare's Lear? Surely it is not that Shakespeare's world is fiction, for what would that make the other? We can not doubt that there is an essential difference, but I shall conclude by doubting that an arbitrary distinction between rhetoric and literature can disclose that difference. Rather, our explorations should be pushed to their natural limits, and those limits may, in many cases, extend well beyond what we anticipate.

FORMAL ANALYSIS IN POETRY AND RHETORIC

Bernard Weinberg

Formal analysis, as applied to literary works, is the art of discovering in any work the basis of its internal organization. Since I think of the basis or principle of internal organization as the "form" of the work, I call the analysis "formal"; and I speak of "analysis" since the process of discovery is one which separates out from the totality of the work a particular element of its constitution.

"Literary works" is a broad and a vague category; and I mean it to be so. For the kind of formal analysis that I have in mind is applicable to a wide range of works, from philosophical treatises, through rhetorical compositions, to poems in all the poetic genres. A philosophical treatise has a "form," and it is usually found in the structure or the organization of the ideas that make up its demonstration. The "form" of a rhetorical composition will consist of the arrangement of its total argument, including the various kinds of pertinent proofs. In any kind of poem, the "form" results from the subordination of all other parts to one dominant part, such as an action or the progressive revelation of a passion. For all works, the "form" is in a very real sense the totality of the work; the process of analysis seeks to perceive the principle upon which that totality is based and to reduce what is discovers about that principle to a clear and comprehensive statement.

But discovery and statement should not, I believe, mark the whole or the end of the analytical process. They should be followed by the particular kind of evaluation for which analysis itself affords the best basis. I am not sure whether evaluation is a by-product of analysis or whether analysis is a necessary step on the way to evaluation; but the kinds of questions that one asks when one inquires into the "form" of a work generate, along with answers about the "form," further answers about the quality of the work, its merits and defects. That is because such questions, in themselves, spring from a conception of what the work might be or should be; they have self-contained criteria; and in most cases an affirmative answer means that the work is "good," a negative answer that it is "bad." When we ask about a philosophical treatise what its first principles are, we should not hope to arrive at an evaluative statement; the only "evaluation" of the first principles must come from a higher philosophy, or from another science, or from the witness of experience. And besides, this is not a "formal" question. But when we ask how further statements are deduced from the first principles, how the logical or the dialectical argument is pursued, in what way the conclusions are derived, we are doing three things at once: we are inquiring into the "form" that the demonstration takes, we are supposing that there are proper or improper ways, good ways or bad ways, of organizing the materials within the given form, and we are pointing toward a conclusion with respect to the successful or the unsuccessful accomplishment of the demonstration. We are combining analysis with evaluation.

For a rhetorical composition, the questions would of course not be the same. I use the phrase "rhetorical composition" because I wish to consider many other types of works than speeches and orations. I wish to include in the category, in fact, any work that seeks to achieve, in a particular audience, a particular effect of persuasion through the use of the various proofs proper to the art of rhetoric. That covers a great deal of territory; it includes many works which one might be tempted to submit to a poetic analysis. Obviously, the questions that one would ask of a rhetorical composition would be entirely different from those suggested for a philosophical treatise. We should still be seeking to discover a form; but a different kind of form, and hence to be sought through a different kind of inquiry. Some questions would necessarily pertain to the internal "form" of the argument, to the kinds of premises and deductions and conclusions used in the persuasive process. But already at this point, while we are still considering internal formal relationships, we should discover that these relationships themselves depend upon the nature of the audience being addressed. In rhetoric, the particular audience is never absent, ever present. Hence many of our questions, and perhaps our first ones, must be directed to a discovery of the character of that audience as it is revealed within the rhetorical composition and as it determines

[37]

all elements of the rhetorical form. Even our questions about the character of the speaker (questions about the "ethical" proofs) will reveal that that character, too, is a "rhetorical" character, made or assumed by the speaker in order to correspond to his conception of the audience, of its expectations or demands, of the kinds of ethical proofs that it would find persuasive. Everything that we ask about the "form" of the rhetorical composition will thus involve simultaneously what goes on "inside" the form and its relationships to an "outside" factor, the particular audience. Once again, the criteria will be built in: to the extent to which the various proofs seem to carry with them the power to persuade the particular audience, to that extent will they be "good."

If the situation in rhetorical analysis is "different" from that in philosophical analysis, it might be said that in poetic analysis it is "opposite" to that of rhetoric. Opposite, primarily, in the sense that whereas all our questions for a rhetorical document lead us "outwards" to the audience that determines the form, all our questions about a poem lead us "inwards" to a form that is essentially self-contained and self-determined. If it is a narrative or a dramatic poem, we shall be brought progressively to the discovery of the action or the plot that organizes all the other elements of the poem, to which all others are subordinated either as causes or as manifestations. If it is a lyric poem, our analysis will lead us to something "like" an action—something that accounts for the movement from the beginning through the middle to the end—even though there may be neither episodes nor characters. This may be a change in the state of mind or heart of the speaker, or his expression of a central passion, or the successive use of devices to play upon the emotions of another. Whatever the case, and whatever the poetic genre, all our questions will be directed to aspects of the internal structure or form; all our answers will reveal interrelationships, or orderings, or subordinations, or causes and effects, affecting all the parts *within* a total form. Evaluative implications will be present each time that we learn something about the degree and the kind of integration of any part into the whole.

You will have noted, I trust, that I said nothing at all about the audience of poetry in speaking about poetic analysis; nor did I mention it in connection with the analysis of philosophical treatises. This was a purposeful omission. For I wished to allow myself the opportunity—which I shall now seize upon immediately—to compare and contrast the roles of the audience in these two areas with its role in rhetoric. Let me begin by saying, in a bold oversimplification, that the audience is entirely absent in a philosophical demonstration, entirely present in a work of rhetoric, and both entirely absent and entirely present in a poem. This is neither a paradox nor an enigma. When a philosopher attends to the making of his demonstration, he thinks only of the validity of his premises and the solidity of his deductions; he is not concerned with what any particular reader, or even readers in general, might think about the "appeal" or the "effectiveness" of his argument. He is working out a logical or a philosophical formula; and let the reader catch up, or catch on, as he can. When a rhetorician (and I mean this in the broadest sense) is composing his work of rhetoric, he thinks first of all about the person or persons to be persuaded, about the likes or dislikes, the expectations, the degree of moral elevation of those persons. These are always particular persons, not a general and universal audience, and to the extent to which he is able to gauge the reactions of those persons, to that extent will he be able to select, from among the "available means of persuasion," the ones best calculated to produce the desired response. Hence the marshalling of his general argument, the passions and the thoughts he chooses to arouse, the things that he deems useful to say about himself, the selection of language, all these will be determined by the character of the audience that he strives to persuade.

When a poet writes his poem, his position with respect to an audience is perfectly clear; it is ambiguous only for us as readers and as critics and as analysts. As far as the poet is concerned, it is not the nature of a particular audience that accounts for his conception of the total form of the poem, for his strategy of organizing and structuring that form, for his choice of the last individual word. I am not speaking, of course, of the poet who is writing a propaganda novel, or a satire, or a play with a social message, but rather of the poet who is writing a novel, or a play, or a lyric with the dominant purpose of writing a novel, or a play, or a lyric—and regardless of what the rhetorical overtones might be. The fact that he is so doing will be evident from the analysis of his poem, from the way in which the parts are organized for their mutual contribution to the whole. His concern will be with the perfecting of the form, not with the "affecting" of a particular audience. Yet an audience will be present nonetheless, and in a very curious way. In spite of the fact that the poet may be seeking no more than the perfection of a poetic form, he will still be hoping, willy-nilly, for something beyond formal perfection, and that is the eliciting of an appropriate artistic response in a reader or a listener or a spectator.

When I say "appropriate artistic response" I refer to a reaction, in part intellectual, in larger part emotional, that reflects the passions and the characters and the moral dimensions within the form itself. The plot of a novel or a play, as it progresses from an initial conflict of personages and situations to a final resolution of that conflict, arouses passions, feelings, sentiments within the persons involved. A lyric is basically the expression of an idea or an emotion in affective terms and through affective devices. In all cases, the emotion or the passion exists first inside the poem, as a cause or a potential for the feelings that will be aroused in a reader. Thus when we ask questions about the form, we are also inquiring, at one and the same time, into the emotional content inherent within the form and into its potential for emotion in whatever audience may contemplate the form. Our analysis reveals, simultaneously, an "effect" built into the poem and an "effect" that will occur in an audience because of what is in the poem. Moreover—and here the situation is the direct opposite of what we find in rhetoric—what happens in the audience happens because of what the poem is, not because of what the audience is. The poet does not begin by determining the character of his audience; he does not proceed by adapting the form of his poems to the peculiar expectations of particular readers. He writes his poem, and if he has written it well, the audience will respond to it as it should, will be subject to the appropriate effect.

This is not a rhetorical effect. It is not an effect of persuasion. It depends neither on the character of a speaker nor on the character of an audience; it contains no proofs—logical or ethical or pathetic. It is an aesthetic effect, one that consists for each poem in the arousal of a specific range of feelings proper to the emotions within the poem. As far as the poem and its effect are concerned, the poet has no "character," no set of moral dispositions that are used by the poet as means to the production of his effect. The audience has no "character," either, no set of expectations or demands or needs that cause the poet to make his poem as he does. Only the poem itself has what we might call a "character," and this is its form.

I have of course stated the opposition in an extreme way, speaking on the one hand of "pure" rhetoric in which all elements of the internal form stem from considerations of the audience, on the other hand of "pure" poetry in which all elements of the internal form are internally determined and where the effect in the audience is a product of the form. For formal analysis, this way of stating the difference means that in the case of rhetoric we must ask questions about the form that will lead to the discovery both of the form and of the external factors that influence it, whereas in the case of poetry all our questions may be directed to discovery of the form itself. As far as the relationship of the form to an audience is concerned, we need ask only whether the form is such that an audience—unspecified and universal—would find it intelligible, whether the passions and the characters and the situations are such that an audience would find them within its normal range of human experience and hence would be able to "feel" them appropriately. In practice, the distinctions are not always so clear and so simple, and the analyst must at times wonder whether he has before him an essentially poetical or an essentially rhetorical work, at times whether a poem is "pure" or "mixed," that is, whether he may limit himself to questions about a poetic form or whether he must add to them questions that he would normally use in rhetorical analysis.

In order to clarify some of these theoretical distinctions, I wish to look briefly at two works of French literature. The first is Flaubert's *Madame Bovary*. It becomes clear, as we read into and through *Madame Bovary*, that we have before us a narrative poem in which most or all of the parts belong to the telling of a story. Our first questions must therefore inquire into the nature of that story and into the ways in which each of the parts contributes to the working out of the story. Our first answers will tell us that Emma Bovary herself is the protagonist of that story, the person centrally involved in the action, and that the action seems to consist, superficially a least, of the passage of Emma from an initial state where she hopes to realize her romantic dream of life and love to a final state where that hope is completely dashed and where, in despair, she commits suicide. The successive episodes in that action are her marriage with Charles (the first hope lost); the ball at La Vaubyessard with its vision of the viscount and of another world; her first platonic affair with the young Léon, in whom she thinks she has found the man who conforms to her dream (his departure destroys the second hope); her seduction by Rodolphe and her first long adulterous relationship, ending again in abandonment and in the destruction of her third hope; her seduction by an older and more experienced Léon who disappoints her both in love and in practical matters (her last hope is thus unfulfilled);

and her death. We have, thus, a view of an external action.

But the asking of other questions about the novel shows that this is an incorrect way of seeing the form, since it does not account for many episodes and for traits of character assigned to various personages. We need, instead, to see an intimate and internal action, one in which Emma, seeking to make life conform to her dream, passes from an initial state of virtue, through successive discoveries of her loss of that virtue, to a final moment where the realization of her complete corruption makes it necessary for her to take her life. In this view of the action, the sequence Charles-viscount-Léon-Rodolphe-Léon is more completely justified, since each relationship corresponds more closely to her state of virtue or morality, her receptivity to vice at the moment; certain episodes, such as her financial dealings with Lheureux, the operation on the club-foot, her visit to the church at Yonville, are clarified as causes of the action; and a whole range of secondary personages, Homais the pharmacist and his helper Justin, the curate Bournisien, the tax-collector Binet, all the known inhabitants of Yonville, take their places as needed elements in the developing story. More important still, this conception of the action permits us to see why each of the personages has the character that is attributed to him, for what purposes particular traits are included, why some need to be rich and constant while others may be simple and passing.

The questions I have asked so far relate to the general form of the action, to the episodes of which it is composed and their sequence, to the persons who participate in it and their characters. I should go on to questions about the things that these persons do and say and why they do and say them; and the answers should be, always, in terms of their relationship to the achievement of the action. I should need, also, to ask about language, about the construction of passages and the choice of words or figures. And why these should be as they are. In all cases, these would be "formal" questions and they would be part of a "formal" analysis; they would be concerned with the components of a poetic form—an action, personages and their characters, passions and ideas, the words used to express all these—and with the way those components are organized into an effective artistic whole.

If, now, we ask the same questions about another work of French literature, Voltaire's *Candide*, we shall begin immediately to get answers that point in an entirely different direction. We do find an overall organizing action, a kind of biographical sequence of episodes

[42]

in the life of the protagonist, Candide. But the order of these events, rather than being determined by any internal narrative necessity, seems either to be haphazard and accidental or to depend upon some external, nonpoetical principle. As we inquire further, we conclude that what we really have is an argument, not an action; it centers about a proposition, "that it is impossible to accept the philosophy of optimism," and proceeds by the accumulation of examples. Every time that the best of all possible worlds appears, it is destroyed; it can exist neither in the old world nor in the new world; the one place where it does exist, Eldorado, is as inaccessible as it is unsuitable to man's nature. The order is thus in part geographical, in part that of a developing thesis: we begin at the Chateau de Thunder-ten-tronck and end in Candide's Turkish garden, and that is because we must begin where everything seems to be for the best and end where happiness really is of a very limited and mediocre sort.

The same conclusions emerge from our inquiry into character. The many personages involved really do not have characters; they represent ideas or points of view related to the main proposition or they provide examples (constantly multiplied) of men and women who have fallen from happiness to unhappiness, from fortune to misfortune. Some of the events and some of the persons, indeed, are even unrelated to the proving of the main proposition. They exist to develop a secondary satire on the devices of the sentimental novel, or a tertiary satire on the institutions of modern European society, or a quaternary satire on Voltaire's enemies and his current *bêtes noires*. The more such questions we ask and the more such answers we find, the more completely we become convinced that the structure of *Candide,* although apparently and superficially poetic, is actually rhetorical. It means to persuade, not only to the adoption of a philosophical conclusion, but also to belief in all kinds of side matters. The action is an argument, the personages are examples or spokesmen. The "effect" is not an emotional participation in a resolving conflict or an emotional response to it, but a kind of belief.

We cannot therefore, as we did with *Madame Bovary,* pursue an analysis that would dig constantly deeper into the workings of a form, but we must instead move into the context of Voltaire's intended audience for *Candide.* We quickly learn many things about that audience—and merely through reading *Candide;* that it is suspicious of metaphysic, dislikes Germans and aristocrats, enjoys *risqué* innuendoes, likes to see Jesuits discomfited, has a sense of the practical and the pragmatic in life and in morals. To please that audience and win it over, Voltaire presents himself (but not directly as would an orator) as sly and irreverent, full of common sense, indignant at nonsense. The "character" of the poet enters in a way that would be improper in *Madame Bovary*, and it becomes manifest through the kinds of things that he chooses to do in writing his rhetorical story, through the way in which he writes it. As we move along in our analysis of *Candide*, we discover that weak and unsatisfactory answers come from questions about its poetic form, but that good and revealing answers come from questions about its rhetorical form. This is a sign that our formal analysis of *Candide* will be most successful if it is directed toward the essential discovery of a rhetorical form and if it studies the superficial poetic form as one of various devices through which persuasion is sought and achieved.

The questions through which we work toward a formal analysis will thus not always be of the same kind. Sometimes, as when we work with philosophical documents, questions will be relatively clear and they will lead to predictable types of analysis. Similarly, works that show themselves upon inspection to be clearly poetical or clearly rhetorical will suggest, almost by themselves, clear-cut questions (appropriate to one or the other structure) that we will ask as means of arriving at answers that will be foreseeable in a general way if not in particular details. For most lyrics or plays or novels, for most speeches or sermons or pamphlets, we may enjoy a sort of pleasant assurance about where we are going (in formal analysis) and how we may most directly get there. But it is in the limbo of the mixed forms, in those works which seem from the outset to partake both of the rhetorical and the poetical, that clarity both of goals and of devices will come only after a long process of testing and rejection. With works such as these, we have no recourse but to try, one after the other, hypotheses that would be useful in poetic analysis and hypotheses that would be useful in rhetorical analysis—and the questions appropriate to each. The form of the analysis itself will emerge as we strive to adapt it to the form of the work, and the firm questions will result from our tentative answers.

Difficulties such as these are particularly acute in the analysis of ambiguous or ambivalent works. But they are found—and they should be found—in the formal analysis of any and every work, in whatever category. Criticism, analysis, evaluation, judgment, these must always remain indefinite and hypothetical; they must never be reducible to formula. Today's reading must leave room for tomorrow's reading, second guessing must always be regarded as superior to first guessing, and we must never regard our ultimate interpretation as anything better than penultimate. For therein lies the joy of the arts of criticism and formal analysis.

CONTEXTUALISM AND THE RELEGATION OF RHETORIC

Murray Krieger

Here is a conference dedicated to exploring relations between rhetoric and poetic. Decorum would require that it proceed out of a mutual respect between these disciplines; indeed academic habit would prompt their mutual inflation. Yet to such a conference I can come only blowing sour notes, even as my sense of the professional occasion leads me to apologize for doing so.

For I come, despite certain reservations that I have several times made in print, as a representative of what I have helped to term "contextualist" literary theory, a dominant theory in recent years. And I must acknowledge—although on this occasion defensively, if not downright blushingly—that this critical tradition can say only negative things about the relation to which this conference is dedicated; indeed it goes further and builds its pedestal for poetry only by making it all that rhetoric (as this theory defines the term) is not. It makes its criterion for poetic failure the work's falling into "mere rhetoric," and it takes its metaphor ("falling into") literally.

So let me be frank. What can a theory do to help us toward relating rhetoric to poetic when it rests on the need to denigrate rhetoric in order to create the very possibility of poetry? One of the major documents in the formulating of this theory, Allen Tate's "Three Types of Poetry," offers not merely the commonplace that poetry is the work of imagination, but the extreme claim supported by the condescending question of W. B. Yeats, "What is rhetoric but the will trying to do the work of the imagination?"[1] What, then, is inferior poetry or pseudo-poetry (as a work of the will) but rhetoric in disguise, poetry that

---

[1] In *On the Limits of Poetry* (New York, 1948), p. 94.

has—to repeat the metaphor—fallen into rhetoric? In this supercilious strain, the hidden refrain, "Alas, poor rhetoric!"

Of course, all that this theoretical tradition creates as its tactic it can create only because it creates and offers us a card-stacked definition of rhetoric; perhaps it is in an examination of this fact that my sort of essay, propelled from the wrong corner, can be of value to this conference despite the denials on which it rests. What, then, is this rhetoric, as these critics so condescendingly use the term? Rhetoric is defined as the use of the available means of persuasion concerning a propositional claim that can be referred to independently of the discourse; which is to say, the claim exists in a complete form prior to the discourse, and it is in no essential way transformed by the discourse. A poem that is termed "mere rhetoric" can be reduced to its means of persuasion, can be treated only as instrument, as device. In short, it is discourse that, however tactically useful, is hardly indispensable. The emphasis on the word "will" as the threat to poetry in Yeats' derogatory definition of rhetoric, with the suspension of the will understood as a prerequisite for the poetic posture, indicates the post-Kantian—indeed almost the Schopenhaurian—sources of this theory. Rhetoric, then, is related to decision and action; poetry, happily, is not. Poetry is related to contemplation and the free play that accompanies it—the contemplation that frees words from their normal semantic and syntactic limitations and that frees our existential world from the contingencies within which our will-driven propensities for action restrict it. Rhetoric is left to employ language in its normal, and normally limiting, way in order to talk about the world within its normally, and willfully, limiting perspectives.

One after another contextualist critic speaks pleadingly of keeping poetry free of the grasp of what is called the "Platonic censor," that which controls nonpoetic forms of discourse. And by Platonic they mean pretty much what they mean when they say "rhetorical." It means the directing of discourse toward something extramural, whether a moral imperative, the claim to a moral truth or to any other sort of truth. So in the dichotomy they draw between poetry and prose or poetry and science—in effect, between poetry and nonpoetry as forms of discourse—the techniques of "mere rhetoric" become identified with poetry's antagonist. Wherever there is a separable and transcendent meaning to the discourse, the discourse becomes translation— "mere" translation, to use again one of their favorite adjectives of derogation. All that can distinguish it as discourse—that is, apart from the value of its separable meaning—is its elegance and its effectiveness, "merely" rhetorical properties both, since neither can transform meaning through its ornamental, "merely" ornamental, devices. In such discourse the form-content dichotomy is seen as complete. But in poetry—ah, poetry!—there is an organic, ever-transforming quality that renders meaning contextually immanent and untranslatable. Meaning uniquely occurs *in* "these words in this order" rather than being carried inviolately (and indifferently) *through* these words as it might be—or has been—carried through others. If the meaning of a poem can be paraphrased—that is, if it can be reduced to a series of propositions—we must hope that we are oversimplifying its totality in our Platonic haste; for if we are not, if our paraphrase, our reduction, really exhausts the meaning of the poem, then we are dealing with poetry of the will, which is to say pseudo-poetry, disguised rhetoric, "mere rhetoric." And our techniques of analysis should become the more modest ones that concern techniques of persuasion, what R. P. Blackmur called "superficial and mechanical executive techniques"[2] (did he almost mean bureaucratic ones?). I have purposely made the contextualists' distinction broadly and in an oversimplified form to make it unmistakable; and I do not argue for it here since it is rather its consequences upon the study of rhetoric and—even more important to me—of poems that border on rhetoric that concern me.

It goes without saying that the contextualist approach carries with it—and quite explicitly—the downgrading of many poems in the accepted canon, especially the allegorical, the satirical, the didactic. For these are all expressly dualistic, indeed referential in their intention, so that what happens in the poem is largely conditioned by demands of an a priori system of meaning—a priori in that it pre-existed this poem and has its authority independently of it. Of course, the tactics of argument may lead the contextualist to say not that he is downgrading what may be termed rhetorical poetry *as* poetry, but rather that he is determining it to be a different sort of discourse altogether, one that demands different techniques and standards of evaluation; that as something else in literature it may be splendid even if it can not create the purely aesthetic occasion that poetry proper can. But this is really no more than a tactical dodge that only mutes the insult if, indeed, it does not aggravate it by an imputation of bastardy.

After I have conceded that entire genres of writing are traduced

---

[2] "A Burden for Critics," in *The Problems of Aesthetics*, ed. Eliseo Vivas and Murray Krieger (New York, 1953), p. 427.

by the contextualist approach, however, I must insist that this approach often opens our awareness to the other than rhetorical dimensions in a poem which we might otherwise think of as mainly rhetorical—dimensions that can convert it into something quite otherwise, a something that rhetorical analysis might never lead us to discover. The "persona" has been a major device that contextualist critics have used to convert rhetorical analysis to poetic. It has been especially effective in converting the rhetoric of self-righteous satire to the double-edged poetic irony of a satirized world viewed by a similarly, if far more subtly, satirized satirist.[3] Thus the revolution in our criticism of Jonathan Swift, most spectacularly of the final book of *Gulliver's Travels*, in which we have learned to treat the Houyhnhnm-loving Gulliver contemptuously, as an imperfect, developing character rather than as Swift's unerring mouthpiece.

I choose Alexander Pope's *Epistle to Dr. Arbuthnot* to demonstrate my point, partly because it is explicitly a verse satire, a traditional—even formalized—satire in general imitation of Horace, and partly because it has received an impressively full analysis as a work of rhetoric.[4] So I choose it mainly because it would seem at the outset to offer so difficult a case—especially when we add the fact that the protagonist and chief speaker in the dialogue is P., obviously Pope, as A., or Arbuthnot, is his interlocutor.[5] Here surely is little room for the fictional ground we would need to convert real author into objectively imagined, dramatically conceived "persona." The poet's respectful attitude to his Arbuthnot assures us that we can take his

---

[3] See Robert C. Elliott, "The Satirist Satirized: Studies of the Great Misanthropes," *The Power of Satire: Magic, Ritual, Art* (Princeton, 1960), pp. 130-222.

[4] Elder Olson, "Rhetoric and the Appreciation of Pope," *Modern Philology,* XXXVII (1939-40), 13-35.

[5] I am assuming, of course, the authority of the Warburton text of 1751, in which the dialogistic attributions to P. and A. are made. There is some question on this point; the Twickenham edition prints the 1739 version, in which the form of the epistle is unbroken except by occasional quotation marks, which often indicate another speaker, sometimes a close friend, with Arbuthnot as a likely candidate. And even its editor, John Butt, acknowledges the possibility that the change from epistle to dialogue was Pope's (Alexander Pope, *Imitations of Horace with An Epistle to Dr. Arbuthnot and the Epilogue to the Satires,* ed. John Butt [London, 1939], pp. 93-94). As a general imitation of Horace, the *Arbuthnot* may be like Pope's "The First Satire of the Second Book of Horace Imitated," which is a dialogue between P. and F., though addressed to Mr. Fortescue. I feel the presence of Arbuthnot is strongly indicated in many of the passages in quotation marks in the earlier version. In any case, the essay by Elder Olson, to which mine is in part addressed, assumes that the poem is a dialogue between P. and A., as in the 1751 version.

attitude to P. as being equally autobiographical and defensive, as fact rather than as fictive reality only. Biographical facts about Pope and his ancestry, the well-annotated enemies he assails make us ever more certain. And, following the lead of the title and the confessional nature of the prefatory Advertisement, we can expand both initials to the full historical names with equal confidence. Thus the poem can only be Pope's *Apologia pro Vita Sua*, his vindication of himself and his purgative role by his self-righteous condemnation of all enemies.

This is surely the unquestioned assumption of Elder Olson who, in his essay appropriately entitled "Rhetoric and the Appreciation of Pope," treats the poem as an effective demonstration of the prescriptions in Aristotle's *Rhetoric*. Olson defines rhetoric in Aristotle as "that faculty by which we are able in any field of discourse to induce belief or conviction in our audience." Pope's art in the poem is defended as the rhetorician's strategy of establishing himself "as a man of good moral character" assailed by unworthy enemies. Olson engages in an impressively detailed analysis of Pope's tactics, from his manipulation of the dialogue form—of the function of that trustworthy witness and interlocutor, Arbuthnot—to his reassurances to the audience of his own tender innocuousness, despite the attacks that increase in fury (from Atticus to Sporus) as Pope wins the confidence of the audience, now secure in their safety from him. Pope answers the attacks of his enemies by justifying his character even as he assumes the role of attacker himself, though an attacker who has delayed attacking beyond all reasonable endurance. Pure though defiled, he persuades us to understand his own defiling at last, even as Arbuthnot does.

Of course, Olson understands that none of this argument proceeds from logic, for the law of its strategy is rhetorical, not logical, as its goal is persuasion, not truth or validity. Thus deception is not only permissible; it is positively to be courted. Every argument in the poem presents us only with circularity since we have only Pope's word for the facts, even for Arbuthnot's presence and for the words that Pope, after all, puts in his mouth. The poem is to establish Pope's good moral character, except that we can trust what he says in it only if we believed to begin with that he had good moral character. It is all dissembling, then, but need be no more for its rhetorical purpose of moving "opinions and emotions," rather than creating a proper response to the demonstration of truth. Saying what he would and acting as he would if he were truly virtuous, he circularly persuades us that he is. He gives us a "semblance" of virtue rather than logical proof of it, the "semblance of truth" rather than truth itself. Imitation becomes a cheat that effectively works its intended way.

Olson would have to acknowledge, then, that our persuasion depends on our taking the fiction for the fact, on the illusion that we are overhearing an actual dialogue, not the "imitation" of a dialogue fabricated for his own interests by Pope. We must, in effect, mistake art for nature—surely not the sort of response the neoclassical writer normally expected of his sophisticated reader who cherished art's artifice. It is the sort of demand, however, that the rhetorical intention demands of its reader, as the poetic—proper imitation seen as but an imitation—does not. All this is the price of Pope's creating his "P." as an ego, not as an objectively created, dramatically conceived *alter ego;* the price of converting poetic imitation to rhetorical persuasion.

Should not this very demand—that the reader be persuaded to forget that he is reading a poem, a free fabrication—put us on our guard against Olson's easy claims that we take the poem for reality in accordance with Pope's strategy? And is it not rather supercilious for Olson to suggest that only a critic as rhetorically wary as he has shrewdness enough to see through the semblance, the deception, and the underlying circularity? As Pope's wit everywhere shows, he was ready to grant wariness to his readers; and any wary reader would surely not be taken in. How many are persuaded by P.'s self-righteous pointing to himself as the injured and the innocent party—especially if we add his contemporary reader's awareness of Pope's reputation for playing a venomous and craftily aggressive public role, a role that Pope would surely trade on? And how many seriously credit the delightful and brilliantly manipulated fiction of Arbuthnot's presence and sympathetic support? To turn A. from character in a dialogue into the breathing reality of Arbuthnot requires as much blindness to the aesthetic fact as he exhibits who would leap onstage to rescue Desdemona from Othello's clutches.

I am not about to invert Olson's claims by saying merely that the poem fails as rhetorical apologetics because of an error in tactics or an underestimating of his reader. Rather I would hold that Pope must have meant to give the game away, that he wanted us to see through the transparent employment of P. and A. and the sometimes painful self-righteousness of P.'s coupling of attacks and self-vindication—to see through these even as we admire the wit that flashes from them. How else to account for what W. K. Wimsatt means when he characterizes the poem as "an exquisite vibration between mayhem and pious professions"? He sees the persona as "a masterpiece of fighting traits justified by benevolent intentions and milky innocence—or mock-innocence (it matters not; in either case, the victims must squirm, and the self-portrait remains in some degree inscrutable)."[6] To what extent has the poet convicted himself and his role as Horatian satirist? given evidence of his own irrationality as well as his rational, justifiably self-righteous superiority over his enemies? I see the conventional Horatian role deepen, the humane being in part overcome by the vicious—the vicious in himself as well as in his enemies, even if we grant that his own viciousness has been inspired and even forced by the attacks of those enemies. Still the put-upon poet becomes, in his forced role within the public arena, the violent man.

Our maturest reading finds P. to be a splendid wit and a dangerous enemy, and thus far to be preferred to his antagonists; but he is also self-deluded precisely where he tries to delude us. And I would claim that Pope means to leave his speaker exposed even as that speaker far more damagingly exposes his enemies. The poet's gladiatorial role is seen critically, even sadly perhaps, although P. is given great freedom to play it broadly enough to appease the appetite of his embittered creator. But the creator is also poet enough to keep P. as the object of a case study. He is transformed from spokesman to persona as the *Epistle* is transformed from rhetoric to poem, from apologia to mock-apologia, at least in part.

But the common-sense likelihoods I began with, that support the biographical equations, are still there, so that evidence of this transformation must be inclusive indeed if our acceptance of these equations and the single satirical thrust is to be shaken. Evidence there is, in the manipulation of both argument and tone: in tactics whose transparency converts them in part to pseudo-tactics and in juxtapositions that shriek their contradictions of motive, compelling our critical awareness of the mixture of violence in innocence.

P.'s primary tactic is to cajole friendliness from his readers through the obvious device of telling them that only the unworthy and the dishonest need fear him: "A lash like mine no honest man shall dread" (303); or, earlier, "Curs'd be the verse, how well soe'er it flow,/ That tends to make one worthy man my foe" (283-4). We are having a distasteful trade proposed to us: say my verse is righteously inspired and I'll say you are worthy or honest. The very act of dreading my

---

[6] "Introduction" to Alexander Pope, *Selected Poetry and Prose,* ed. William K. Wimsatt, Jr. (New York, 1951), p. xlv.

lash is an admission of your guilt; so protect yourself by defending my verse. But P., in his anxious display of self-righteousness, must overstate his case to the point of disingenuous sentimentality. His verse is to be cursed, not only if it makes one worthy man his foe, but (he goes on) if it should "Give virtue scandal, innocence a fear,/ Or from the soft-ey'd virgin steal a tear!" (285-6). If the reader is not aware that he is being put on in the first of these couplets (283-4), this second of them, with its deadpan piety, would seem to make it unmistakable.

P. uses the sentimental and the pious in many places to proclaim his sanctity. There is the repeated invocation to "thee, fair Virtue," as his goddess, to whom his satires are at all costs dedicated and who oversees the bitter sacrifice her servant willingly undergoes. And if he must be impolitic even where it is politically dangerous, his goddess prompts the indifferent priggish pronouncement, "A knave's a knave, to me, in ev'ry state" (361). Self-satisfied by the "pious professions" Wimsatt spoke of, P. can continue with his justified "mayhem." Where his own person enters, piety and sentiment come with it and together they introduce a cloying self-pity as well. I can cite, as an obvious example, his reference to "this long disease, my life" (132), the "being," "preserv'd" by Arbuthnot, which the poet must manage to "bear" (134). Another and more extended example is his introduction of his gentle parents, innocent, maligned by his enemies, one dead and the other kept awhile "from the sky" (413) only by the poet's dutiful and loving solicitude.

But insidious juxtaposition appears here, as well, to give the game away. P. begins by defending the unslanderous natures of his parents: Why are they slandered? ". . . that father held it for a rule, / It was a sin to call our neighbour fool; / That harmless mother thought no wife a whore: / Hear this, and spare his family, James Moore!" His pious defense of his slandered parents as non-slanderers ends in slander, with P.'s implying the gossip that James Moore Smythe was a bastard. Don't you insult my family, who are innocent and who, in their honest simplicity, would insult no one, not even your family who deserve the insult I hereby give them!

This device of contradictory juxtaposition is the poet's defense against being taken only seriously by us, his indication to us of his self-critical awareness. He uses it frequently. Often he will join disarming modesty about his poetic talents with implied confessions of genius. The phrase "many an idle song," which he uses to describe

[53]

his works in a sentimental couplet ("Friend to my life! [which did not you prolong, / The world had wanted many an idle song]," 27-8), occurs just two lines after the conjunction of "wit, and poetry, and Pope." This conjunction has all the world's ills blamed on him as the sole incarnation of the twin spirits of wit and poetry. Or where he apologizes for falling involuntarily into the harmless and soothing art of poetry to help him bear this long disease, his life, he lists those distinguished writers whose praise encouraged him. His conclusion is hardly in the soft tones: "Happy my studies, when by these approv'd! / Happier their author, when by these belov'd! / From these the world will judge of men and books, / Not from the Burnets, Oldmixons, and Cookes" (143-6). Here his name-dropping (Granville, Walsh, Garth, Congreve, Swift, Talbot, Somers, Sheffield, Atterbury, and Bolingbroke) has led to a braggadocio awareness of his talents.

The momentary modesty of claims about himself, related to his half-meant retreats to soft sentimentality and like them undercut by a tougher scornfulness, is related also to his protestations of his patient endurance of ill-treatment. And ironic juxtapositions occur here as well. He can proclaim his humility with a sequence of examples that concludes with his charge of plagiarism against his enemy, James Moore Smythe: "So humble, he [P. himself] has knock'd at Tibbald's door, / Has drunk with Cibber, nay has rhym'd for Moore" (372-3). His humility turns into his pride in being copied, his docile nature into an aggressively charging one. Yet the transformations are masked by the parallel order which presents his being victimized by the plagiarist as an act that is graciously voluntary on his part ("has rhym'd for Moore"). The irony in the juxtaposition totally undercuts the soft pretension. Or earlier, answering charges that he has written barbs that were really fashioned by others, P. seems to be at once above reproach, cocky, and arch: "Poor guiltless I! and can I choose but smile, / When ev'ry coxcomb knows me by my style?" (281-2). Here we have his half-meant claim of innocence ("Poor guiltless I!") together with his awareness of his inimitable satiric style and his hidden acknowledgment that his own barbs, well-sharpened and directed, have earned him everyone's anxiety—hardly a consequence of innocence, of guiltlessness. Guiltless he is, in these particular cases; but he is mistaken to be guilty—as he implicitly admits—only because he has been so guilty, and so brilliantly and so often guilty, elsewhere. Thus while insisting upon his soft-hearted endurance of violent opponents, he clearly admits to retaliating in kind: "Were others angry:

I excus'd them too: / Well might they rage, I gave them but their due" (173-4). And after describing one after another of his dunces, he concludes with the claim and counter-claim, "All these, my modest satire bade translate, / And own'd that nine such poets made a Tate" (189-90). "Modest satire" indeed!

It is the act of attacking while denying he has the temperament to attack that constitutes the basis for these contradictory juxtapositions. Can Pope not wish us to ask how the P. who speaks his brilliant and damaging lines in the poem can also characterize himself as "soft by nature, more a dupe than wit" (368)? Are you serious? The words burst from us, if we have been observing P. at all carefully. As we have repeatedly seen, he represents himself as one who would excuse —has excused—his enemies, although he insults them on all levels, public and private, lightly and gravely, even as he parades himself as resisting the urge to do so. We have observed how the excusing of those who rage (173) is coupled with his giving "them but their due" (174). Through the use of indirection, the tongue-in-cheek contradiction takes back his claim in the very act of his making it.

The boldest example is, of course, the Atticus portrait in its relation to the disclaimers that precede it. In the preceding verse paragraph P. has been giving the dunces their due, arriving at the summary couplet, whose mixed quality we have noted: "All these, my modest satire bade translate, / And own'd that nine such poets made a Tate" (189-90). His modesty is answered by rage: "How did they fume, and stamp, and roar, and chafe! / And swear, not Addison himself was safe" (191-2). Is he? Well, P. follows by opening his next line with the unqualified assurance, "Peace to all such!" What follows, of course, is the portrait of Atticus, with its almost unveiled attack on Addison. This daring conjunction of protestation and vituperation is mockery indeed. The wounded innocence of "Peace to all such!"—as if I would touch *him*—joins with the thin disguise of the code name Atticus and with the contrary-to-fact condition of the extended subjunctive construction that follows as the portrait ("But *were* there one . . ."). What makes the disguise not merely thin but utterly transparent is the fact that Pope knew his readers, as followers of the arena of public poets, would know and recall: that the Addison portrait had appeared some dozen years earlier without disguise. How in keeping with the complex nature of P.'s satire here that in being assimilated to a new whole the formerly discrete portrait follows so misleading a preamble.[7]

---

[7] Both the 1722 (perhaps unauthorized) and the 1727 versions of the portrait,

P. may indirectly be reminding the reader, through the portrait of Addison and the history of feuding it recalls, that the current poem is hardly the first time that its author, creator of *The Dunciad* (referred to on line 79), has been on the offensive, despite his pious protestations of innocence, of a desire to live outside the arena: "Oh, let me live my own, and die so too! / (To live and die is all I have to do:)" (261-2). These lines of simple and soft retirement lead to others: "I was not born for courts or great affairs; / I pay my debts, believe, and say my pray'rs" (267-8). This subliminal awareness of his prior role as assailant is to qualify the central and continual assumption that the self-righteous P. appears to be urging: that except for the assault he is launching *now*—at the very moment of composing this poem, at the very moment of his claiming not to be launching it, not to be temperamentally able to launch it—except for this one time he has resisted launching it. How, then, this poem?—unless he is using the paradox of its being, its curious status, to reveal the uproariousness of his soberer claims, to reveal the fact that he is toying with us and with his satirist's role.

At one of the poem's more naked moments of self-exaltation, P. is describing the ideal poet (guess who), what he avoids and what he seeks. (For example, "Not proud, nor servile, be one poet's praise," 336.) What he does, including his satirizing, the moralizing of his song, he does "not for fame, but virtue's better end" (342). Are we to believe in this selfless, disinterested service of the goddess? Or are we to recall the more damaging implications of the earlier line 127: "As yet a child, nor yet a fool to fame"? As a self-poclaimed servant of virtue, he still is not a fool to fame, then? My point must be, it should by now be clear, that in playing the game, in writing this very poem as he has written it, he does become one. And the

---

printed long before its inclusion in the complete *Arbuthnot* in 1734-35, refer to "A—n" instead of "Atticus." While the first puts the portrait in no significantly broader context, the second ("Fragment of a Satire") not only is very close to the final version in *Arbuthnot*, but is also preceded by lines very similar to the preamble we have examined. But one of the differences is crucial—and most helpful to my argument. Just before "Peace to all such" we find "How would they swear, not *Congreve's* self was safe!" How significant to replace Congreve, a respected ally Pope would not attack (see *Arbuthnot*, line 138), with Addison, the very figure immediately to be attacked. Could Pope have made such a substitution—from a name that claimed his innocence to one that proved his guilt—without a keen awareness of a changed strategic purpose which the satiric portrait of a poet now a decade and a half dead was in the final version made to serve? For the earlier versions, see Alexander Pope, *Minor Poems*, ed. Norman Ault, completed by John Butt (London, 1954), pp. 142-145, 283-286.

earlier line indicates his half-knowledge of the fact. He proves that he has become a fool to fame by the very act of claiming—in the ways we have seen him claiming—not to be one. But he becomes one necessarily, through the aggressive need to defend himself, to show himself as self-righteous, protector of the role of poet become Horatian satirist-rhetorician in the degrading and self-degrading public arena. But the poet has remained to remind us of his saving critical consciousness of that role and its demands, demands that have caused him to be victimized into writing his apologia.

Thanks to his continual tongue-in-cheek qualification of this angry defense, our double view of P. tempers the rhetorical with the poetic, so that the element of mock-apologia ends by leading to a far profounder apologia; one based on an understanding of the pressures, the appeals, the temptations of the public poet's arena, its rivalries and hatreds, its inhumanities, and the human response to it as well as the rationalizing—if transparent—defense of that response. He may be the best of poets (and surely he is trying to persuade us of this as well, I am free to admit) but, as *The Dunciad* tells us, it is the worst of times. There is, then, a final sense in which the flight from rhetoric or transcendence of rhetoric leads to a rhetorical purpose after all, so that poetics may be seen to have its rhetoric or rhetoric its poetic. This possibility opens the way for—indeed demands—a new and far subtler, far more flexible and even poetic, definition of rhetoric than Aristotle's. But that would be the subject of another, and a far more difficult, essay than this one—one that would be friendlier and more fitting to the union of disciplines that is the proper objective of this conference.

Let me admit, by way of epilogue, that, partly out of my engagement with polemic, I have meant somewhat to overstate my case for the persona, thus rendering clearer than they are the confusing, and probably confused, elements in a poem that is too much a collage. In my own defense I point out that I have tried throughout to insist upon the doubling of our rhetor-poet's voice, his bitterness at others as well as his self-awareness, except that I have not sufficiently pressed the unsystematic, sporadic nature of this doubling. My further methodological confession, then, is that I have meant to follow Pope's lead, learning tactics from his tactics, as in my employment sometimes of the first and sometimes of the third person in speaking of the contextualist. For, like Pope, I have meant to insist upon the limitations of my perspective even as I have tried to exploit it for all the ad-

[57]

vantages it could provide, thus rendering myself attack-proof even as I deepened my attack—by including myself in its swath. But such confessional candor in motive-hunting is the subject for yet a third essay.

THE BEGINNINGS OF PROSE TRAGEDY

Marvin T. Herrick

The beginning of prose tragedy in western Europe has been generally assigned to George Lillo's *London Merchant* (1731), which did represent a radical break with the usual practice of tragic dramatists. Ever since the fifth century B.C. tragedians usually selected a historical or legendary tale of royal or noble characters involved in a heroic disaster and then wrote a play in high-sounding verse. As the prologue to the *London Merchant* announced, Lillo's play was to be "in artless strains, a tale of private woe." While this bourgeois tragedy was scarcely artless, it was certainly an unpretentious tale of common, ordinary people, and it was written in prose.

Lillo's prose, however, seldom got very far away from the traditional blank verse, and it retained some of the old-style inflated rhetoric that went back as far as Seneca. Especially in highly emotional passages Lillo was apt to shift into iambic pentameters. Two examples will illustrate this phenomenon.

In the third act, Lucy says,

> Oft he in anguish, threw his eyes towards Heaven,
> and then as often bent their beams on her. (3.4)

In a later scene in the same act Barnwell says to his dying uncle, whom he has just stabbed:

> O, do not look so tenderly upon me!
> Let indignation lighten from your eyes,
> and blast me ere you die! —
> By Heaven, he weeps in pity of my woes. (3.7)

As George Nettleton[1] has observed, "Judged by the modern stand-

---

[1] *The Cambridge History of English Literature* (1939), X, 86.

ards of prose drama that has felt the influence of Ibsen, Lillo's prose is sheer travesty."

Lillo apparently lacked the courage to pursue the new path he had blazed with the *London Merchant*, for he turned back from prose to verse in his next bourgeois tragedy, *Fatal Curiosity* (1736). But we cannot dismiss the *London Merchant* as an accident that bore no fruit. In 1753, Edward Moore brought out another prose tragedy, *The Gamester*. More important, both Lillo and Moore strongly influenced better playwrights on the Continent, notably Diderot in France and Lessing in Germany. With the establishment of the *drame* and the *bürgerliches Trauerspiel*, prose tragedy gained at least a foothold on the European stage.

The experienced student of the drama, or of any other art for that matter, should not be content to accept Lillo's play as the first appearance of prose tragedy—not until he has checked the Italians. If we go back to the formative years of modern drama we may expect to find some forerunners of Lillo, Moore, Diderot, and Lessing in Italy. And so we do. Italian experiments in prose tragedy appeared as early as the middle of the sixteenth century.

As Bernard Weinberg[2] has shown, the literary quarrel over Sperone Speroni's *Canace*, a neoclassical tragedy of incest read by the author to the *Accademia degl' Infiammati* of Padua in 1541 or 1542, first printed in 1546, explored the whole range of tragic theory and practice from ancient to contemporary times. The most important critical document in this quarrel was *Giuditio sopra la tragedia di Canace e Macareo, con molte utili considerationi circa l'arte tragica e di altri poemi con la tragedia appresso*, first printed at Lucca in 1550.[3] The *Giuditio* is in dialogue form. During the discussion of the proper language for tragedy, one of the speakers asks why the Italian playwrights, who had long been seeking a conversational style and had all but given up rhyme for the dialogue, should not go another step beyond unrhymed verse and write prose tragedy. The author's spokesman, a learned Florentine, dismisses this query by stating that Aristotle considered verse an essential part of tragedy.[4] While this answer seemed to settle the matter at the time, the possibility of prose tragedy was posed.

Long before 1550 Italian playwrights had successfully overridden

[2] *A History of Literary Criticism in the Italian Renaissance* (Chicago, 1961), pp. 912-953.
[3] The author was almost certainly Bartolomeo Cavalcanti.
[4] *Giuditio* (Lucca, 1550), 35r.

objections of the Ancients and established prose as the language of comedy. Although there was no unanimous acceptance of this departure from the practice of Plautus and Terence, and some comic writers continued to use verse throughout the century, most Italian comedies were written in prose. It was almost inconceivable, however, that the tragic cothurnus could appear on stage without the accompaniment of high-sounding verse—almost inconceivable, but not quite. Cicero was esteemed as fine an artist as Virgil or Terence. Moreover, some serious religious plays began to appear in prose. These *sacre rappresentazioni*, however, were not accepted by the learned as true tragedies.

About the time that the quarrel over Speroni's *Canace* was developing, that is, about 1546,[5] Francesco Negro, a former Benedictine who had become a militant Protestant, published a play called *Tragedia intitolata Libero Arbitrio*, which soon had a fairly wide circulation. It was translated into French at Villefranche in 1558, into Latin at Geneva in 1559, and about thirty years later into English as *A certayne Tragedie wrytten fyrst in Italian, by F.N.B. entituled, Freewyl, and translated into Englishe, by Henry Cheeke.* This so-called tragedy was written entirely in prose.

Negro's play is neither a right tragedy nor a right *rappresentazione sacra,* but a hybrid form partly medieval and partly neoclassical. It has most of the mechanical features common to neoclassical drama: it has five acts divided into scenes; it starts in *medias res,* on the day that the news of the Protestant revolt in Germany reaches Rome; all the scenes take place in a Roman piazza, and the action occupies only one day. On the other hand, many of its characters suggest a morality, for example, the apostles Peter and Paul, the archangel Raphael, a king named Free Will, a secretary named Human Discourse, a steward named Unlawful Act, and Signora Gratia Giustificante (Lady Grace Justifying).

Why did Negro presume to call his religious play a tragedy? The apostle Paul explains why to a barber.

But doest thou know Bertuccio in what case this kyng [Free Will] standeth? I wyll tell thee howe, euen in the same case that kings stand in tragedies rehearsed upon a stage: for many times the poorest and vilest man, appeareth there in the apparell and fourme of a kyng, and seemeth to haue great power and many seignories, but in deede al is but a faigned and

---

[5] Ferdinando Neri, in *La tragedia italiana cinquecento* (Florence, 1904), p. 126, says that the first edition of Negro's play was printed in 1546-47; but I know of no copy that early. The Illinois copy is the second edition of 1550.

fabulous thing. Imagine therefore my Bertuccio, that this world is a stage, where the deuyl wil set forth a fable of a certayne kingdome, which he calleth the kingdome of good workes.[6]

Libero Arbitrio is almost a travesty of contemporary Italian tragedy. King Free Will is a sorry hero; he appears only briefly on stage in one scene (2.1), but loses his head in the last act to the sword of Grace Justifying—offstage in the approved neoclassical manner. The real hero is the humble barber, Bertuccio, who is a character out of Italian comedy. The author was primarily concerned with Protestant propaganda, not with arousing and relieving the emotions of pity and fear. His play is actually much closer to the Latin Christian Terence, that large body of school plays that dramatized biblical or religious stories in the form of Terentian comedy, than it is to either Italian tragedy or the Italian sacred drama. I suspect that Negro's principal model was the Latin tragedy of *Pammachius* (1538) by Thomas Kirchmeyer, a German admirer of Martin Luther. Nevertheless, under the guise of tragedy, *Libero Arbitrio* did introduce prose dialogue in a serious play, and we may profitably look at two samples of this prose.

Early in the first act, a pilgrim called Fabius is talking about the instability of Fortune, a favorite subject of tragic poets from Seneca to the imitators of Seneca in the sixteenth century. Such talk was usually couched in formal language, often embellished with figures of speech. Notice how Fabius proceeds.

Qualunche volta l'huomo è stato longo tempo felice, signore Diaconato, egli puo et debbe espettare in brieue qualche contrario caso, percio che questa è la natura de l'instabile fortuna di fare ciascuno in questa vita et de suoi beni et de suoi mali scambieuolmente partecipe.

Although a man haue long continued happy, yet (maister Diaconatus) he may and ought to looke shortly for some contrary chaunce, for such is the nature of unconstant Fortune, to make every man partaker in this life as wel of her yll, as of her good.[7]

While this passage is not artless, it is far removed from the customary tragic discourse about fickle Fortune, and moreover it is hardly the high style of Ciceronian prose.

Negro did not remove all the mythological allusions that abound in Senecan tragedy. Nor did he forego all figures of speech. His literary allusions and figures, however, are more often biblical than classical,

---

[6] *A certayne Tragedie . . . Freewyl* (n.p., n.d.), p. 131.
[7] Cheeke's translation, p. 5.

and invariably they are homely. The following exchange between Atto Elicito and Bertuccio will illustrate my point.

At. Questa prouincia per certo cape gran moltitudine di brigata. Non penso per mia fe, che l'Egitto de suoi frutti senza pioggia producitore, hauesse mai ne tante rane, ne tante locuste al tempo di Faraone.
Ber. Anzi costoro che l'habitano sono essi medesimi locuste, et sono di quelle, che Giouanni nella sua reuelatione vide gia uscir fuori dell'abisso. Ma sequitate Notaio.
Act. Surely this province holdeth a great multitude of people. By my fayth, I think Egypt which bringeth forth fruite without rayne, had neuer so many frogges nor Locustes in the time of kyng Pharao.
Ber. In deede those which inhabit it are Locustes, for they are such as S. Iohn in his reuelation sayth, he saw come foorth of the bottomlesse pit. But proceede maister Notarie. (p. 41)

While I am not suggesting any direct connection between *Freewyl* and the *London Merchant*, it is curious to observe that the sixteenth-century Italian anticipated and went beyond the familiar prose of the eighteenth-century Englishman. Certainly Negro's prose is further removed from verse than is Lillo's.

Over forty years after "Free Will" and the *Giuditio* appeared, namely in 1592, Agostino Michele published a *Discorso* "in which, contrary to the opinions of all the most illustrious writers on the art of poetry, it is clearly shown how comedies and tragedies can be written in prose with much praise." And the author proceeded to practice what he preached; he wrote a prose tragedy which we shall examine a little later.

Meanwhile Giambattista Velo wrote *Tamar*, "a tragic action presented in the city of Vicenza, by the New Company in the year MDLXXXVI."[8] This play is all in prose except the prologue and the choral odes, which are in unrhymed verse. When the chorus takes part in the dialogue it speaks prose.

Velo's use of prose here, however, was accidental, not deliberately planned. In an address to the reader appended to the printed version, the author explained that he was forced to use prose because the play had to be written in a few hours and because some of the actors could not manage verse. Every literate person, he admitted, knows that "tragic matter ought to be written in verse."

Tamar, which combines the story of Amnon's rape of his sister Thamar with Absalom's rebellion, is not a good play; but its chief

---

[8] Printed at Vicenza in the same year, 1586.

fault does not lie in the style. Although Velo's models were the Roman Seneca and the Italian Giraldi Cinthio, who was an imitator of Seneca, his rhetoric is almost never Senecan; he abandoned bombast and virtually abandoned mythological allusions and highfaluting figures of speech.

The opening speech in *Tamar* is Bathsheba's complaint about fickle Fortune. Her style is scarcely more elaborate than that of Negro's character.

Bene, ahi lassa, conosco, che alcuno felice, o beato chiamar non si puo; mentre in questo carcere di miserie si trova (1.1).

I know truly, alas, that no one can be called happy or blessed while he is still in this prison of miseries.

Later in the same scene Bathsheba has an opportunity to hold forth on the onerous duties of her husband the king. Her speech here is far from artless, but again it is straightforward and relatively simple.

Poi che non solamente il Principe di se stesso pensar deue; ma della casa propria, della Città, del popolo, et in somma di tutto quello che sotto la sua protettione si troua.

For the Prince ought not only to think of himself, but of his own house, of the city, of the people, in short of all that is under his protection.

Even in crucial scenes, for example, in scenes wherein messengers report sensational disasters, on which Seneca and his Renaissance followers lavished their finest rant, Velo restrained himself. (Since he was writing for untrained actors, perhaps he had to restrain himself.) The servant who reports the suicide of Achitophel in the third act starts his account in a manner reminiscent of the Senecan *nuntius* and the Italian *nuntio*.

Dove ne vado ahi lasso? come da me fia raccontata si dolorosa nova? con quali parole esprimer potro sí horrible successo? che solo a ramentarlo tutto d' horrore pavento (3.4).

Alas, where am I going? How may I recount such grievous news? With what words will I be able to express such a horrible event? For in merely recalling it I am overwhelmed with horror.

He soon calms down and proceeds with a matter-of-fact report of how Achitophel hanged himself from a beam in his study.

More dramatic and much more highly charged with emotion is Chusai's report in the last act of the battle between loyalists and rebels. David is most anxious to know what happened to his favorite son. Chusai replies to his query:

Absalone (et spiacemi a dirlo) è giunto a quel termine a che ogni mortale
eternamente è prescritto. (5.2)

Absalom (and I am sorry to say it) has arrived at that end to which every
mortal is eternally destined.

The language here is as plain as that of the original account in the
Old Testament.[9]

David begins his lament:

Ohimè, o caro, o caro figlio, dunque dunque sei morto? O crudelissimo
colpo, che con il traffigere il corpo del figliuolo, hai anco traffitta l'anima
del padre, o lugubre vittoria, o più d'ogni altro sanguinoso conflitto.

Alas, O dear, dear son, then, then you are dead? O most cruel blow that in
piercing the body of the son has also pierced the soul of the father! O
mournful victory, O combat bloodier than any other!

This lament is reminiscent to some degree of the wailings in Senecan
tragedy, but the extravagant figures and the studied conceits that so
often appear in such speeches are absent.

Even the chorus in *Tamar*, at least when engaged in dialogue, is
temperate.[10] In the third act, Bathsheba has convinced herself that
ruin for the whole royal family is imminent. The chorus of women
tries to comfort her.

Dopo il bene il male; et dopo il male, il bene succeda pero nelle prosperità
si deve temere; et nelle avversità sperare. (3.2)

After good evil; and after evil good may succeed; therefore one should fear
in prosperity, hope in adversity.

So it goes throughout *Tamar*. Velo's language is almost as plain

---

[9] The *Bibia volgare* (Venice, 1566) reads: "Alqual rispondendo Chusi disse,
i nemici del mio Signor re, et tutti quelli si levano contra di esso in male siano
fatti come il putto."

[10] The choral odes in verse are naturally more poetical. The following extract
from the ode at the end of Act 2 is typical:

> Questa vita mortal che a tanti, e tanti
> Mali soggiace ogn' hora,
> (Quasi Nave tra l' onde, e venti posta)
> Par che giammai si fermi
> In un stato medesimo; e i giorni, e l' hore,
> E i mesi, e gli anni sono
> Sempre penosi, e sempre
> L' un mal succede all' altro. . . .

It seems that this mortal life, which submits every hour to so many many evils
(like a ship placed between waves and winds) never stays still in the same order;
and the days and hours and months and years are always painful, and always one
evil succeeds another.

as Negro's in *Libero Arbitrio,* and more readable.

Ten years later, in 1596, Agostino Michele's experimental tragedy entitled *Cianippo* was published at Bergamo. Michele was content to follow the practice of most neoclassical tragic poets in taking his argument from the history of ancient Greece and Rome. In this instance he chose the nineteenth section of Plutarch's *Parallel Histories of Greeks and Romans,* specifically the story of Cyanippus of Syracuse, who neglected sacrifices to Bacchus and paid for this neglect by ravishing his only daughter in a drunken stupor and then losing his life at the hands of this daughter. Michele departed from neoclassical practice in writing all of his tragedy in prose except the brief choral odes at the ends of Acts 1 to 4. Even the prologue, delivered by the god Bacchus, is in prose.

The style of *Cianippo* is actually a step backwards by comparison with *Tamar;* that is, Michele's prose is more studied, less familiar than Velo's. Michele did his best to rival the high style of tragedy, but he chose Cicero as his model instead of Seneca. The result is relatively free from mythological allusions and bombast, but no one can say that it even suggests artlessness. On the contrary, almost every speech is contrived; many are carefully balanced, antithesis abounds, and so do amplifications. No character is exempt from an artful rhetoric; the servants speak as carefully as do the king and princess.

The following extract from a speech by Bacchus in the prologue will illustrate the carefully balanced periods of Michele.

Sopportar dunque più non debbo, che la mia Deità dal mondo tutto perch' è buona amata, perch' è possente riverita, perch' è giusta temuta sia, da te solo Cianippo hor vilipesa, biasmata, calpestata. . . . Son io forse di minor grado fra gli Dei in cielo, od a loro d' inferior possanza fra gli huomini in terra? la mia gratia non ti è stata cara, non ti è stato grato il mio amore, ti sarà nimica la mia ira, e ti sarà avversario il mio furore, e provarai tuo mal grado quanto possa giustissimo sdegno d'un Dio contra la vana et sciocca alterezza d' un huomo mortale (1v-1r).

Therefore I ought no longer to tolerate that my divinity which is well loved by the whole world, mightily revered, justly feared, should now be despised, reproached, trampled upon by you alone, Cianippo. . . . Am I perhaps of minor rank among the gods in heaven or with less power than theirs among men on earth? My favor has not been esteemed by you, my love has not been acceptable to you; my wrath will be your enemy, and my fury will be your adversary, and despite yourself you will show how much the most righteous scorn of a god may be able to do to the vain and stupid pride of a mortal man.

[66]

The learned counselor, a character out of Seneca, might be expected to use elegant speech. So he does. Notice the amplification in his remarks to the high priest:

Come la Natura ha sciolto ogni legame al mio pensiero; affine che liberamente dir io vi possa, che Bacco non con la guerra come Marte, non con la pestilenza come Diana, non con la sterilità come Cerere, non co' l fulmine come Giove, ma solo col vino punir ci puote(4r).

Since nature has loosed every bond from my thought, so I may freely tell you that Bacchus cannot punish us with war as does Mars, not with pestilence as does Diana, not with barrenness as does Ceres, not with the thunderbolt as does Jove, but only with wine.

The old nurse's speeches, while simpler than the passages quoted above, are as carefully arranged. When the old woman first hears of the rape she is profoundly shocked and can only exclaim in broken wails. But she soon settles down into balanced periods.

Che cosa orribile odo io? ohime infelice. Ditemi, dolcissima figliuola mia, come? quando? dove? da cui? O cielo, perch' acconsenti a malvagità si grave? O terra, perchè si abbominevol mostro patientemente sostieni? (13v).

What horrible thing do I hear? O me unhappy! Tell me, sweetest daughter, how, when, where, by whom? O heaven, why do you assent to such noisesome wickedness? O earth, why do you suffer patiently such an abominable monster?

In her last speech, when Ciane lies dead by her own hand, by the same bloodstained dagger she used on her father, the nurse carefully preserves her artful style.

Ah dolcissima figliuola mia già queste poppe vi diedero per tributo il latte; hor quest' occhi vi consacrano le lagrime, e tosto queste vene vi conduceranno in sacrificio il sangue. Vi diedi il primo cibo nella vita vi daro l' ultime esequie nella morte(40r).

Ah sweetest daughter, these breasts once gave you their milk in tribute; now these eyes hallow my tears for you, and soon these veins will bring my blood in sacrifice for you. I gave you the first nourishment in your life, I will give you the last funeral rites in your death.

One more illustration from *Cianippo* must suffice, namely, a bit of rather good dialogue which sounds like everyday speech and yet is certainly artful. Late in the fourth act, Ciane learns from the priest who her ravisher is. Of course the priest does not know that there has been a rape, but he knows the owner of the man's ring that the princess had found in the dark underground passage.

Sacerdote: Dirollovi volontieri perch' è conoscente vostro.
Ciane: Io lo conosco?
Sacerdote: Non sol lo conoscete, ma con sommo ossequio lo riverite.
Ciane: Ahimè io lo riverisco?
Sacerdote: Anzi che non pur lo conoscete, e lo riverite, ma non men che voi stessa l' amate.
Ciane: Ahimè misera, ahimè infelice io l' amo?
Sacerdote: Cianippo padre vostro, e Re vostro, ha l' annello come suo a me chiesto, et allui da me l'annello, come suo, è stato restituito (30v).

Priest: I will tell you willingly because he is an acquaintance of yours.
Ciane: I know him?
Priest: Not only do you know him, but you revere him with the highest respect.
Ciane: Alas, I revere him?
Priest: In fact, not only do you know him and revere him, but you love him no less than you love yourself.
Ciane: Aye-me miserable, aye-me unhappy, I love him?
Priest: Cianippo your father, and your king, has asked me for the ring as his, and the ring has been returned by me to him as his.

Evidently Michele's attempt to establish prose tragedy in Italy was not successful.[11] Comic playwrights continued to use prose and writers of tragicomedy adopted prose, but the Aristotelians remained inflexible in their opposition to prose tragedy. Over half a century after Michele's *Cianippo*, Giovanni Battista Filippo Ghirardelli, a *letterato* whose name has been kept alive by Corneille's favorable notice in the *Discours de la tragédie*,[12] offered a long wearisome tragedy entitled *Costantino* at Rome.[13] Ghirardelli used no verse at all, and he abolished the chorus.

The Aristotelians, headed by one Ippolito Schiribandolo, at once damned the play. The author defended himself in a discourse even longer than his tragedy. The main objection of his enemy was based on the conviction that Aristotle considered verse an essential part of tragedy and that many generations of Greek, Latin, and Tuscan poets had used only verse in tragedy.

---

[11] Eee Emilio Bertana, *La tragedia* (Milan, n.d.), p. 217.
[12] In referring to the Italian tragic dramatists, Corneille spoke of "un de leurs plus beaux espirits, Jean-Baptiste Ghirardelli."
[13] The first edition was printed in 1653 at Rome. A second edition with the author's defense of his tragedy was published at Rome in 1660.

Logically, Ghirardelli's answer to Schiribandolo sounds reasonable enough. He argued that Aristotle did not maintain that verse was the measure of a poet, that Herodotus in verse would still be a historian, not a poet, because, unlike Homer, he was not an imitator, not a maker of plots. Neither verse nor prose, said Ghirardelli, is an essential part of tragedy: "Verse, therefore, is only an ornament, not the soul of poetry."[14] Furthermore, and with some justification, Ghirardelli pointed out that the unending experiments by such notable Italian dramatists as Trissino, Giraldi Cinthio, Lodovico Dolce, and Sperone Speroni to find a conversational style in tragedy had failed. "Short, broken verse *(il rotto)*," he argued, "is too comic and humble; all blank verse *(l'intero sciolto)* is too harsh and difficult; all rhyme is too sweet and unrealistic *(inverisimile);* the *sdrucciolo*[15] is too limping *(cadente)* and subdued; and a mixture of all these too unseemly and diverse."[16]

Ghirardelli may have had theory on his side, but his own practice was not calculated to win followers, and the Aristotelians remained in power. Prose did not rejuvenate the tragic stage in seventeenth-century Italy as leadership in the European drama shifted from Ferrara, Florence, and Venice to London and Paris. George Lillo, whose use of prose in tragedy was hardly so far advanced as that of Italians nearly two hundred years earlier, still remains the most influential pioneer of modern prose tragedy. It was Ibsen, however, who, for better or for worse, clinched the victory for prose tragedy in the fall of 1873 with the publication of his *Emperor and Galilean*. In January of 1874, Ibsen wrote to Edmund Gosse, who disapproved of his abandonment of verse: "The illusion I wished to produce was that of reality . . . . By employing verse I should have counteracted my own intention . . . . We no longer live in the days of Shakespeare."[17]

---

[14] See *Difesa . . . dalle opposizioni fatte alla sua tragedia del Constantino* (Rome, 1660), p. 46.

[15] The *sdrucciolo* is an unrhymed verse ending in a dactyl.

[16] *Difesa*, pp. 61-62.

[17] *The Collected Works of Henrik Ibsen* (New York, 1909), V, xv.

PROBLEMS
IN
SPEECH
TEXTS

Richard Murphy

At the outset, let me doff my cap to the general theme of the conference, and then plunge into one particular aspect of the subject. My specific theme, "Problems in Speech Texts," may suggest textual criticism with attention to *recensio* and *codex unicus*, archetypes and hyparchetypes, *examinatio*, with particular attention to Indicative Errors and Stemmatic Types—or perhaps even a learned application of the textual methods of Paul Maas[1]—that great German authority—to the texts of Senators Humphrey and Goldwater in the recent campaign. But my intention is much less ambitious—it is to look into some of the major problems of getting a fair copy of a speech, discovering what sort of copy it is—whether stenographic, predelivery, revision by author, revision by editor or someone else, accurate or inaccurate, complete or incomplete—and to draw some conclusions about the kind of attention and appreciation we should give to various kinds of texts. Applications are mainly to American and British sources. These remarks will probably strike my colleagues on the panel and the professors emeriti as rather naive, but I hope will impress the younger graduate students as fairly sophisticated—especially since little has been written generally about these matters. There is, of course, the very practical treatment, "Establishing The Authenticity of Texts," in Thonssen and Baird's *Speech Criticism*,[2] and Loren Reid's "Factors Contributing to Inaccuracy in the Texts of Speeches,"[3] contained in the little paperback of significant studies put together by

---

[1] Paul Maas, *Textual Criticism*, trans. Barbara Flower (Oxford, 1958).

[2] Lester Thonssen and A. Craig Baird, *Speech Criticism* (New York, 1948), pp. 297-311.

[3] Donald C. Bryant (ed.), *Papers in Rhetoric* (St. Louis, 1940).

[70]

Mr. Bryant in 1940. And there is Walter W. Stevens' "Inaccuracies in the Texts of Congressional Speeches,"[4] with particular attention to deletions of profanity from the *Congressional Record.*

Acknowledgment should be made, however, to some of the fine work in textual criticism, especially on earlier texts. There is Dorothy Bethurum's treatment of eleventh-century homilies, *The Homilies of Wulfstan,*[5] in which all extant MSS sources are compared, and special attention is given to audience adaptations and to "oral" figures and tropes. Or, on the same man, Dorothy Whitelock's *Sermo Lupi Ad Anglos,*[6] "The Sermon of the Wolf to the English"—the title is Latin but the text Anglo-Saxon—in which five MSS are compared. The note on line 40, for example, reads, "H omits *hus* and a fifteenth-century hand has added *bybode* above the line." "H" is Bodleian MS.343, formerly N E F. iv. 12, fol. 143 v. ff., a mid-twelfth century collection of homilies. The Potter and Simpson[7] volumes—ten in number—of Donne's sermons should also receive a nod of acknowledgment, and also K. J. Fielding's *The Speeches of Charles Dickens,*[8] the most zealous attempt to establish readable texts I have seen. These examples are in contrast to the usual treatment of a speech text in collected works of speakers or in anthologies, where the nature of the text is seldom noted or its basic source identified.

Some attempts have been made to establish what was actually said in a speech. An example is the work on the Kennedy-Nixon debates, *The Great Debates.* In that volume, Clevenger *et alii* note the various significances of a speech text and the need for accuracy:

. . . the text of a speech is a multi-dimensional document, limited only by the number and variety of points of view from which it is approached. To certain analysts it becomes a set of linguistic structures; to others a source of information about the values and issues of a period; to some investigators it is an index to the behavioral patterns of a society; to others a vehicle for evaluating the speaker, his ideas, his style. In this sense, each analyst perceives a different speech, because each treats a different kind of data. Yet all are working with different aspects of the same concrete event, and the extent to which each analysis will be valid and meaningful depends upon the accuracy of the text.[9]

---

[4] *Central States Speech Journal,* XV (Aug. 1964), 183-188.

[5] (Oxford, 1957).

[6] Dorothy Whitelock (ed.), *Sermo Lupi Ad Anglos* (London, 1939), p. 27.

[7] Evelyn M. Simpson and George R. Potter (eds.), *The Sermons of John Donne* (10 vols.; Berkeley, 1953-1962).

[8] (Oxford, 1960).

[9] Theodore Clevenger, Jr., Donald W. Parson, and Jerome B. Polisky, "The

There are many motives for reconstructing a speech text other than for textual criticism.

Before going further into the problems of speech texts, let us define what a speech is. A speech is a verbal composition (usually in prose—although there have been sermons composed in verse) of variable length, fashioned for a specific or a generic audience, usually but not necessarily spoken and frequently but not always listened to, in which are interrelated author, reading or listening audience, theme, and occasion, for the purpose of directing the reader or listener to a conclusion selected by the composer. In its practical form, such as salesmanship or soul-saving, a certain amount of success in effect is anticipated. If a speech is to become literature in the broadest sense, it must be written or recorded in some way on brain, paper, wax or tape for transmission and examination and appreciation; it should have qualities of ethical appeal and universality, moving force and fluency, an artistic design, and humane value. In the speeches which have become literature, whether Burke on conciliation with the American colonies, Lincoln at Gettysburg, or Woodrow Wilson on the League of Nations, a certain amount of failure in immediate effect has been traditional.

I give this definition because there is a contemporary movement to look upon a speech as some existential form,[10] fleeting sound and movement, something like a dance, a moment in history, not to be repeated or preserved. Contemporary speakers seem sympathetic to this notion, and show less and less concern for their compositions; so when some mildly excellent speech is made and recorded, such as Kennedy's Inaugural, it is regarded as a phenomenon. And rhetorical critics give less and less attention to texts, preferring "live rhetoric." So the "earnest graduate student in speech makes, in current jargon, a 'rhetorical analysis' of 'a specific speech, delivered to a specific audience, on a specific occasion, for a specific purpose,' showing, among other things, how the 'speaker' adapted to his audience, without the student's having the slightest notion of what he is working on."[11]

I am assuming that a speech text may exist independent of actual

Problem of Textual Accuracy," in *The Great Debates,* ed. Sidney Kraus (Bloomington, 1962), p. 341.

[10] For further treatment of this concept, see my "The Speech as Literary Genre," *QJS,* XLIV (April, 1958), 117-127.

[11] Quoted from my "On Collections of Speeches," *Central States Speech Journal,* XII (Autumn 1960), 57.

delivery or even an actual audience. The speech is a form of discourse, and exists as such. There is no reason why authors should not write speeches and hide them in a trunk even as Emily Dickinson wrote poems and hid them away, except that writers of speeches are more eager for plaudits of the multitude than are poets. The speech is personal expression; it is a sort of public diary. It is studied for *ethos,* traits of character overtly expressed, and as evidence of consistent value judgments by the speaker. The novelist, the historian, the song writer, the epic and dramatic poet may exist only incidentally to their compositions. But the speech is regarded as a lyric, as a specimen of personal thought and feeling revealed in public. There may be expository or narrative passages in a speech that could stand alone when excerpted, but generally the first thing asked about a speech is, who said this? And what sort of person is he?

I

Now to the problems. I want to discuss three general textual problems not peculiar to speeches but significant and persistent. After that, I will take up five textual problems peculiar to a speech as a form of discourse. The first of the common textual problems is sheer accuracy in printing copy of whatever it is that is being printed. In that little volume which classes in British Public Address have had to rely upon for years, *British Historical and Political Orations,* edited by Ernest Rhys in the Everyman's Library,[12] in Chatham's speech "immedicable *p*ulnus" for "immedicable *v*ulnus," (incurable the wound) has gone through various reprintings since 1915 and a revision in 1960. In Bacon's "Speech Against Dueling," which students and I have read together for years in Brewer's *The World's Best Orations,*[13] there is the expression, "the dog to be *eaten* before the lion," which we have pondered for meaning. Finally having recourse to an earlier text, I discovered the phrase is "the dog to be *beaten* before the lion."[14] This makes sense in the context, which is that in government sometimes the lesser rather than the greater person should be admonished and made an example of. Inaccuracy in copying or printing is, as I say, not peculiar to speeches, but it is a problem in the texts, and an old one. In the tenth century Aelfric prepared two volumes of ser-

---

12 (London, 1915; reprinted 1924, 1933, 1950). Title of the revised edition is *British Orations from Ethelbert to Churchill* (1960).
13 David J. Brewer (ed.), (St. Louis, 1899), I, 198.
14 *The Charge of Sr. Francis Bacon, Kt. His Majesties Attourney General, touching Duels* (London, 1670), p. 1.

mons to be copied and read in the churches. He charged the scribes to be accurate:

I now pray and implore, in the name of God, if any one will transcribe this book, that he carefully rectify it by the copy, lest, through negligent writers, we be blamed. He does great evil who writes false, unless he rectify it, as though he brought the true doctrine to false heresy; therefore should every one correct that which he had perverted to wrong, if he will be guiltless at God's doom.[15]

A second problem not peculiar to speeches is finding the best copy. Let me exhibit this handsome plaque of President Kennedy's Inaugural Address as issued by the Government Printing Office[16] and distributed in quantity by senators and representatives. It is a quality job of three-tone printing, but alas, the text leaves something to be desired. There are thirteen deviations from disc and tape recordings I compared it with—such variations as "are found around the globe," for "surround the globe." The copy is identical with that given in the *Congressional Record*,[17] but may have been taken from the GPO *Inaugural Addresses Of The Presidents Of The United States*,[18] which used the *Record* text. An accurate copy of what was actually said, except for one editorial change, could have been found in Kennedy's collection of speeches, *To Turn The Tide*.[19] The government catalogue says the plaque is "suitable for framing."

A third problem, more prominent in speeches than in other forms of discourse, but not peculiar to them, is completeness. Speech anthologies abound in bits and snatches. Something more than accuracy—editorial judgment—is involved here. Some speeches seem to go on forever, whereas the pearls can be strung in relatively few lines. In his final volume of *Representative American Speeches*, published by H. W. Wilson in "The Reference Shelf,"[20] A. Craig Baird—and I nod to "himself" in the audience—ran Richard Nixon's "Checkers Speech," but not all. The editor made a tape of the talk, but evidently felt enough was enough, and humanely substituted four dots for what would have been the final page. The problems of completeness and editorial discretion are not easy ones. Excerpting or compressing for many speeches would be an act of kindness. But how does the reader

---

[15] Benjamin Thorpe (ed.), *The Homilies of the Anglo-Saxon Church* (London, 1846), II, 3.
[16] Catalogue No. 88-2: H. doc. 190.
[17] January 20, 1961, 970-971.
[18] (Washington, 1961), pp. 267-270.
[19] (New York, 1962), pp. 6-11.
[20] (New York, 1953), pp. 72-82.

know what agonies he has been spared? Manager Bryant is editing a volume of British speeches. He and his four subeditors have sworn a mighty oath that all texts shall be complete, or if not, any deletions shall be noted as to extent and nature of materials. But this is a promise, not yet a production.

II

Now to turn to those problems peculiar to speeches. First is the problem of recording what someone else says. True, authors other than speechmakers sometimes dictate. If Homer was transmitted orally for centuries, someone had eventually to write him down or recite to a scribe. Blind Milton dictated poems to his daughters, and some present-day authors use some sort of dictaphone device, but in the main, writers write. But when a speech is pronounced and written down, there is the problem of hearing accurately and recording accurately. Cleveland Amory heard Senator Goldwater's introducer in Madison Square Garden say, "We are going to make the White House the *White* House once again," and so recorded it in *Saturday Review*. But the introducer protested he had said "the White House the *Light* House."[21] Gibbon, the historian, was much pleased to have Sheridan, in the Hastings trial, refer to "the luminous page of Gibbon." But asked how he had come upon such a felicitous phrase, Sheridan replied he had really said "VO-luminous."[22] When Daniel O'Connell complained to a reporter that a speech had been bungled, the reporter claimed he had been caught in a shower and many of his notes had been washed away. O'Connell replied it must have been a remarkable shower to wash away one speech and substitute another.[23] In 1962 General Douglas MacArthur gave a speech at West Point which was variously reported. *Life* ran the speech in a cover-story when the general died this year.[24] Although he had not entirely faded away in 1962, his articulation and pronunciation were hard to follow. At one point he told the Cadets they were "the leaven which binds together the entire fabric of our national system of defense." But he pronounced "leaven," *leeven*, and the word was reported in one text as *leever*, meaning *lever*.[25] As another example of the prob-

---

21 Cleveland Amory, "First of the Month," *Saturday Review*, XLVII (August 1, 1964), 5.
22 Harry Graham, *The Mother of Parliaments* (London, 1910), p. 282.
23 *Ibid.*, p. 283.
24 LVI (April 17, 1964), 36-38A.
25 Professor Otto Loeb Dieter, University of Illinois, has an extensive collection of tapes and prints of the MacArthur speech, and has supplied me with these examples.

lems of transcribing speeches, there are the Lincoln-Douglas debates of 1858. Edwin Erle Sparks, in his edition of the debates, described the "difficulties under which the reporting was done—the open air, the rude platforms, the lack of accommodations for writing, the jostling of the crowds of people, and the occasional puffs of wind which played havoc with sheets of paper." In a note on human frailty he says: "Quite naturally the Democratic reporters did not exercise the same care in taking the exercises of Mr. Lincoln as with those of Mr. Douglas, and vice versa."[26]

The hazards of reporting parliamentary speeches—so many of them are numbered among the greatest, Chatham, Sheridan, Burke—are not always recalled by students who study what we have in the way of texts. It was not until 1907 that an official, verbatim report of speeches in Parliament was provided. Prior to that time there were summaries and improvisations, but with no standard of textual accuracy. So we are dependent in many instances on the diaries of Sir Simon D'Ewes or James Rushworth—described by Carlyle—"Rushworth's huge Rag-fair of a Book; the mournfullest torpedo rubbish-heap, of jewels buried under sordid wreck and dust and dead ashes, one jewel to the wagon-load. . . ."[27] In other instances we have fictionalized versions of great parliamentary speeches. Dr. Johnson composed the texts of parliamentary speeches in the *Gentleman's Magazine* from 1740 to 1743, although he visited Parliament only once, and his authorship was not generally known until after his death. He had his quiet moments of amusement; when in 1777 two speeches on spirituous liquors bills by Lord Chesterfield were published, Johnson is reported to have said: "Here now are two speeches ascribed to him, both of which were written by me; and the best of it is, they have found out that one is like Demosthenes, and the other like Cicero."[28] Because of opposition to having debates reported—to this day when you as a stranger visit Parliament you must sign a paper that you will take no notes—transcribers went through many inconveniences. Charles Dickens, once a shorthand reporter, observed: "I have worn my knees by writing on them in the old gallery of the old House of Commons; and I have worn my feet by standing to write in a preposterous pen in the old House of Lords, where we used to be

---

[26] E. E. Sparks (ed.), *The Lincoln-Douglas Debates of 1858* (Springfield, Ill., 1908), p. 82.

[27] Thomas Carlyle, *Oliver Cromwell's Letters and Speeches*, I, Introduction.

[28] Benjamin Beard Hoover, *Samuel Johnson's Parliamentary Reporting* (Berkeley, 1953), p. 44.

huddled together like so many sheep. . . ."[29] Dickens worked in a relay of reporters. After sessions, "he and his fellow reporters, who had been spelling each other in three-quarter-hour shifts, would repair to a little tavern in the Palace Yard. Here, in an upstairs room kept sacred to their use, they would write out their copy and compare doubtful passages with colleagues who had sharper ears."[30] An exasperating aspect of accuracy in recording is the way the relative accuracy of text differs for any one speaker. Oliver Cromwell had his speech on the dissolution of Parliament, January 22, 1654, taken down in shorthand, transcribed, and he himself corrected it for printing by Henry Hills, Printer to His Highness.[31] However, in a later speech of April 15, 1657, there was no provision for recording. Unofficial diarists Burton and Smythe could not see to take notes, the hall was so dark. They conferred with another unofficial diarist, Rushworth, and found he was in the same predicament. They went to old Oliver to see what he could recall, but he "could not remember a word"[32] of what he had said. So the speech went unrecorded.

Trying to set down accurately what someone else says is one aspect of textual accuracy, but what if the reporter is satisfied with something less than completeness or accuracy? In many cases the intent is not to record an accurate copy of a speech, but merely to report the substance. Those handsome leather-bound volumes of parliamentary debates English, Scots, and Irish squires subscribed to in the eighteenth century were accounts of what happened in Parliament and not recordings of what exactly was said and how it was said. In 1790, there appeared a pamphlet honestly titled, *Substance of the Speech of the Right Honourable Edmund Burke, in the Debate on the Army Estimates, in the House of Commons.*[33] Many speeches were so issued, whether plainly marked or not, simply as the *substance* of the speech. And then there were the devices to avoid accuracy, such as reporting in the third person, a practice still carried on in England. "He was not prepared at this time, the Prime Minister said, to make a definitive statement, but perhaps later in the day something might be said. He regretted many of the insinuations, he added." Now try-

---

[29] Edgar Johnson, *Charles Dickens* (New York, 1952), I, 62.

[30] *Ibid.*, p. 64.

[31] Wilbur Cortez Abbott, *The Writings and Speeches of Oliver Cromwell* (Cambridge, Mass., 1945), III, 594.

[32] Charles L. Stainer (ed.), *Speeches of Oliver Cromwell 1644-1658* (London, 1901), p. ix.

[33] (London).

ing to put together a speech from such indirect incompletions is a job for Dr. Johnson. The origins of this device I do not know. It is a way of working incomplete text into a story, or perhaps the main virtue is exemption from libel since the speaker is not directly quoted. Imagine the difficulties of working with a poet's text such as this: "The world is too much with us, Mr. Wordsworth observed, adding that if this tendency continued, late and soon, in getting and spending and all that, we might lay waste our powers, or something to that effect."

This first problem peculiar to speeches, setting down accurately what was said, might seem to be enough. There is a second problem, how to cast what was said in a form suitable for permanent record. One aspect of this problem is slips in phrase or diction, valuable for students in linguistics, but annoying to the speaker and posterity. General MacArthur, in the speech at West Point previously referred to, spoke of "the mire of shell-shocked roads"—that is what he said. Obviously he meant "shell-pocked roads," and the *Assembly,* published by the Association of Graduates, United States Military Academy, so printed it.[34] But *Life* stuck to "shell-shocked." Edward VIII, in his abdication speech, misread the line, "I have been comforted by Her Majesty, my Mother, and by my Family," by saying "and by her (family)," but corrected himself. In all printings of the speech Robert W. Smith[35] examined in his study of the address, this misreading was ignored, perhaps for common courtesy, perhaps because copy for the press was supplied.

Another problem in preparing copy for permanence comes in correcting inaccuracies and illiteracies. The first edition of the Lincoln-Douglas debates was printed from copy supplied by Lincoln—it was his scrapbook which is now in the Library of Congress. The clippings on Lincoln were from the Chicago *Press and Tribune,* a Republican paper, and the coverage of Douglas was taken from the Chicago *Times,* a Democratic paper. Lincoln wrote to the committee which sponsored the printing that the debates were "as reported and printed," . . . his (Douglas's) by his friends, and mine by mine." He had made, Lincoln said, a few changes, but "verbal only, and very few in number."[36] But Douglas complained in the later editions that

---

34 XXI (Summer 1962), 14-15.
35 "Rhetoric in Crisis: The Abdication Address of Edward VIII," *Speech Monographs,* XXX (November 1963), 335-339.
36 *Political Debates Between Hon. Abraham Lincoln and Hon. Stephen A. Douglas* (Columbus, 1860), p. lv.

Lincoln had corrected his copy without giving Douglas a chance to do so—a critical point since Lincoln was regarded by many as an illiterate backwoodsman.

In the good old days of Burke, and Gladstone, and Lord Morley, speakers were supposed to be able to compose orally, and to get out of a sentence with grammar and syntax intact. But reliance on notes and manuscripts, on teleprompters and idiot boards has corrupted us, and studies and examples I have seen indicate most of us are practically illiterate (by standards in writing) when we talk. Recently a student of mine did a dissertation on oral and written forms.[37] He asked ten people in the Department of Speech to select an article they thought was representative of their best writing. He then interviewed them on the topic covered in the article. I was one of the subjects, and was amazed to discover on looking at his transcription of my oral, impromptu remarks, that I was on the other side of literacy. Eisenhower was celebrated for his syntactical anarchy, but *Time*[38] ran samples of his and Kennedy's press interviews, with identifications printed upside down at the bottom of the page, and there wasn't much choice as to syntax.

Another tendency in printing speeches is to revise for improvement in style and content, for preservation by posterity. All those nice local allusions, such as to guests on the platform, highly recommended in the beginning speech textbooks, are deleted in the search for universality. The closer a speech is designed according to practical standards of success set forth in the textbooks, the greater the revision will have to be. When my colleague, Marie Hochmuth Nichols, prepared for publication her lectures on rhetoric and criticism delivered at Louisiana State University in 1959,[39] she was joshed about making so many changes. What would these compositions be, she was asked, and how should they be described? The LSU Press catalogue answered this question by describing the lectures as "polished for publication," and on the dust jacket they were described as "thoughtful and urbane essays." When Hugh Blair wrote down his *Lectures on Rhetoric and Belles Lettres,* he probably did the same thing. You recall he published the lectures after he retired from the

---

[37] Joseph Anthony DeVita, "Quantitative Analysis of Comprehension Factors in Samples of Oral and Written Technical Discourse of Skilled Communicators" (Ph.D. dissertation, Department of Speech, University of Illinois, 1964).

[38] LCCIX (January 26, 1962), 18.

[39] *Rhetoric and Criticism* (1963). The catalogue referred to is *Spring Books 1963.*

chair in 1783, and in self-defense. Over the twenty-four years of his lectures at Edinburgh, so many student copies were circulated, he noted in his Preface, he thought it necessary to record what he actually wanted to have said. (This was long before the publish or perish era.) A copy of the lectures made by one John Bruce in 1765,[40] records Blair as having said, "Among all the various talents which Providence has bestowed on Man, there is none more eminently usefull (sic) than that which serves for the transmission of thoughts." Blair in published form reads: "One of the most distinguished privileges which Providence has conferred upon mankind, is the power of communicating their thoughts to one another." The lady or the tiger? What did he say? Although what Lincoln said at Gettysburg is still something of a mystery, there is a rough copy in his handwriting which he probably held in hand as he spoke. He made four copies at the request of collectors, and the speech got better and better. For example, the first draft reads, "This we may, in all propriety do." The final copy reads, "It is altogether fitting and proper that we should do this." Facsimilies of the five copies were published last year in *Long Remembered*.[41] Lincoln's changes were few but significant. Many speakers have made gross changes in speeches before publication. Lord Rosebery studied Lord Randolph Churchill's speeches as published and as extant in manuscript. He concluded that Lord Randolph, in editing his own speeches, "omitted from those volumes many passages which might cause personal annoyance, or which did not seem to stand the test of time and reflection."[42] A contemporary problem in revisions is found in reports of debates in the Senate, where, as most people know, the senator or his legislative assistant may make corrections in the reporter's copy if he catches it before it goes to press in the *Congressional Record*.

Problems of accuracy in recording, problems of editing for permanence, and now a third problem peculiar to speech texts, the non-delivered speech. What to do with it? It's not a speech, say the existentialists; it wasn't delivered. In the House of Representatives, a member may "revise and extend his remarks" in the Appendix and so have included in the record a speech that he never made. But there are more notable speeches that never get delivered. Milton never

---

[40] This copy in longhand is in the Strong Room of the University of Edinburgh Library. This is the opening sentence of the two-volume work.

[41] David C. Mearns and Lloyd A. Dunlap, *Long Remembered* (Washington: Library of Congress, 1963).

[42] Lord Rosebery, *Lord Randolph Churchill* (New York, 1906), p. 102.

intended to deliver his *Areopagitica,* although he wrote it as a speech and called it a speech. In 1780, the Earl of Buchan wrote a speech to be delivered at a special meeting of the peers of Scotland. The peers didn't meet, but Buchan had his speech ready, had it handsomely printed,[43] and dedicated it to his brother, Thomas Erskine. Mark Twain was scheduled to speak at a luncheon after the christening of a ship, but the ship couldn't be loosened from the ways, and the whole thing was called off. When the ship finally was launched, two weeks later, Twain was on his way to Europe, but his speech was published.[44] At the height of his career Senator Joseph McCarthy released a sensational speech on the menaces of Communism, and it was front-paged in the papers,[45] but he was so busy he never did get around to giving it. And alas, we can add to this list of undelivered speeches a manuscript prepared for delivery before the Dallas Citizens Council and the Dallas Assembly. It was published in the *Congressional Record,* November 27, 1963.

Problems of accurate recording, editing for permanence, what to do with the nondelivered speech, and now a fourth problem peculiar to speech texts. This is the synthetic text, assembled from various versions. To illustrate Jeremy Bentham's book of fallacies, Sydney Smith put together "Noodle's Oration,"[46] an assortment of bits of parliamentary reactionary rhetoric. Chauncey Goodrich, in his *Select British Eloquence,* blended several versions of Strafford's speech at his impeachment in order to get the most satisfactory text. Mr. Fielding, in his collection of Dickens' speeches I have mentioned, set out to make a variorum edition showing all possible variations in texts, but ended by supplying a single text with notes on what the various sources were for any one speech text. This old problem was noted in a now famous passage from Thucydides:

With reference to the speeches in this history, some were delivered before the war began, others while it was going on; some I heard myself, others I got from various quarters; it was in all cases difficult to carry them word for word in one's memory, so my habit has been to make the speakers say what was in my opinion demanded of them by the various occasions, of course, adhering as closely as possible to the general sense of what they

---

[43] *Speech of the Earl of Buchan, Intended to have been Delivered at the Meeting of the Peers of Scotland, for the General Election of their Representatives, October 17, 1780* (Edinburgh, 1780).

[44] *Mark Twain's Speeches,* ed. Albert Bigelow Paine (New York, 1923), pp. 164-167.

[45] See newspapers for November 9, 1954.

[46] *The Edinburgh Review,* XLII (August 1825), 386-389.

really said.[47]

So, when your hear Pericles speaking at Ceramicus Cemetery, 431 B.C., remember Thucydides wrote the papyrus roll-prompter.

A fifth textual problem peculiar to speeches is the interrelation of kinds of texts and the purposes for which they were used. On rare occasion there may be a text of what actually was said. There may be a predelivery text handed out to reporters, and sometimes a supposedly stenographic copy, done perhaps by stenographers accompanying a presidential candidate. There are texts and partial texts by newspaper reporters and spectators who hoped they heard and recorded aright. There may be in the speaker's archives a copy of the MS he read from, with corrections and additions, whether spoken or not. If the speaker is famous, or his speech becomes so, then there will be the revised printed version. Interrelating all these texts is something like collating medieval MSS of parchment, except you do not know quite what you are looking for. My office is in a building called Lincoln Hall. For years a bronze plaque of the Gettysburg Address, about six feet by six, was set in the floor of the main entrance. The tradition was that no one was to tread upon it, but after a half-century the bronze letters were worn smooth, and it was mounted in the entrance wall. Now suppose you were to choose the version to be so perpetuated in bronze. Would you select the first, that nearest actual delivery, practical rhetoric, or the last, that nearest poetic? And why?

CONCLUSION

Perhaps some tentative conclusions may be drawn from all this. First, we can say that every attention should be given to getting an accurate copy of what was actually said. This is desirable for sheer accuracy, for one thing. It is necessary for interpretations; historians must rely considerably on speeches in discovering the past. It is necessary for linguistic studies and examination of oral forms. As MacEdward Leach has written in his article, "Problems of Collecting Oral Literature":

As you run through the standard collections of songs, tales, proverbs—folklore of the past—you discover that almost without exception it was collected with little reference to how it was originally presented. It is invariably collected as if it came from written sources, as if it were eye literature rather than ear literature. Since it was collected as eye literature, it is edited and judged as written literature.[48]

---

[47] Thucydides, *The History of the Peloponnesian War*, Bk. I, chap. 1.
[48] "Problems of Collecting Oral Literature," *PMLA*, LXXVII (June 1962), 335.

How true this is! Even Percy's *Reliques* are recorded in written version, although all credit to the redoubtable bishop for rescuing the MS from the fireplace. Have we not now reached the point in history where anything other than an accurate tape recording is unsatisfactory as a record of what was actually said?

No less real, however, is a text which has been revised and improved. If a maker of a speech wishes to recollect in tranquility, and improve his composition, why should he not do so? We permit revised editions in other forms. Were Lincoln alive today, he might get into the textbook racket, and keep revising his text to meet the latest syllabus requirement. Required materials for Speech 1863, only the latest revision of the address will suffice.

We shall have to accept the nondelivered speeches and the composite speeches and the burlesque speeches (such as the Eisenhower Gettysburg Address burlesque)[49] if they are compositions in speech form. They are no less speeches than many ramblings given before an audience, often not speeches at all in form.

We shall have to accept most of our speeches of the past as fiction, to be read and studied much as we would a fictionalized biography. There is Patrick Henry's "Liberty or Death" speech, 1775. Baird, in his collection, *American Public Addresses*, prints a version of the speech. He notes that the speech as we have it was composed by William Wirt, some fifty years after delivery. The speech is clothed, Baird says, in literary, almost poetic language. The movement and style are not to be found in any other speech by Henry; and then he asks this definitive question: "How far are we to rely on this text as an authentic Henry recording?"[50] There is a vast literature of fictionalized speeches; in fact most of our preserved speeches are fictionalized versions. Much futile argument goes on about texts which can never be verified. Logan's Oration, 1774, was supposedly delivered by the Mingo Indian Chief just off Ohio-U.S. Highway 23 between Circleville and Chillicothe.[51] He refused to attend a white man's conference, but spoke a speech to an emissary, who took it down. First published by Thomas Jefferson, it was printed by McGuffey in his 1866 *Reader*, and by Houston Peterson in his 1956 edition of *The World's Great Speeches*. Theodore Roosevelt gave five

---

[49] See Oliver Jensen, "The Gettysburg Address in Eisenhowese," in *Parodies*, ed. Dwight Macdonald (New York, 1960), pp. 447-448.

[50] (New York, 1956), p. 29.

[51] See Ray H. Sandefur, "Logan's Oration—How Authentic?" *QJS*, XLVI (October 1960), 289-296.

pages in his *The Winning of the West* to a study of the speech's authenticity, and concluded it was "authentic." "Doubtless there have been verbal alterations in it," he wrote, but "there is not extant a report of any famous speech which does not probably differ in some way from the words as they were actually spoken."[52] Why worry about authenticity of fictionalized speeches? Why not read them for what they are, always aware that they are not recordings of what was said? Are Jane Austen's novels to be examined as documentaries?

One of the frustrating experiences in tracing speech texts as to what was actually said, is that it is impossible to discover much. In written manuscripts, yes. Dead Sea Scrolls are discovered in caves in jars, but remote are the chances of digging out of the ruins in Northumbria a tape on which is recorded the famous sermon of Bede when the angels descended and chanted, "Very well done, thou most venerable Bede." I remember once I was working on a speech by Theodore Roosevelt, "Biological Analogies in History," given at Oxford in 1910. T. R. wrote the speech before he went to shoot lions in Africa, and sent the MS to the Oxford Press. As a courtesy, on the day he delivered his speech, there was a ceremony at the press, and his speech, printed and bound, was presented to him, an hour before he was to deliver it, and he read from the printed copy."[53] It turned out the speech was too long, and T. R. cut here and there. What did he say? I got the insane notion of trying to find out. According to press accounts he was presented his copy by R. W. Chapman, Secretary of the Board of Delegates. I came across a description in an Oxford newspaper of what pages Roosevelt had skipped. So I consulted Chapman to verify all this, and he informed me he was not at the ceremony, and he further advised me never to try to discover what a speaker had actually said. A magnificent try at reconstructing the past was made by Loren Reid several years ago. He traced variations of William Pitt's last speech, 1805, only a sentence long. He found many variations, no accurate copy, and decided Macaulay probably came closest in an article in the *Encyclopaedia Britannica:* "Let us hope that England, having saved herself by her energy, may save Europe by her example."[54] Most of what has been said, or left unsaid, is gone forever. It is difficult to believe that with all his thundering, John Knox left only one sermon recorded, and that was by a historical

---

[52] Chap. IX.

[53] *Biological Analogies in History* (Oxford, 1910).

[54] Loren Reid, "The Last Speech of William Pitt," *QJS,* XLIX (April 1963), 133-137.

accident. On August 19, 1565, he preached at St. Giles' in Edinburgh and made some reference to Jezebel. Mary Queen of Scots took the remarks personally, and banned Knox from further preaching. In frustration he wrote down his sermon, noting in his preface that he left out some things but none touching on the dispute.[55]

Another conclusion, and this is very spooky—it has to do with ghosts. The ghost writer has been with us a long time, but with a difference. When Lysias or Isocrates or Demosthenes wrote a speech for somebody else to deliver, he still claimed the speech as his own. The Athenian ghost was a body, a somebody. The ghost now, however, is as spooky as Halloween. The ghost is a real problem in studying speech texts. Ernest R. May, writing in *The American Scholar*, has delineated some of these problems. He says:

> The choice and order of words in Jefferson's writings enabled Adrienne Koch and others to rebuild and portray his pattern of thinking, but for contemporary figures similar analysis is practically impossible. If, on the basis of letters and speeches, a scholar should try to analyze Franklin Roosevelt's mind, he would emerge with a figure made up of Roosevelt and the fragments of Roosevelt's ghosts—Rosenman, Sherwood, Michelson, Grace Tully, Missey Le Hand, even the sprightly apparition of Harold Ickes.[56]

This is an old problem. Does Washington's "Farewell Address" represent him or Alexander Hamilton, who may have written it? Perhaps one answer to the problem is to restore the ghost to Athenian status. This was done the other day when *The Wall Street Journal*[57] headlined: WILSON PROMISES BID TO NATIONALIZE STEEL FIRMS SOON. The story said: "The pledge came in the Queen's speech, written by Prime Minister Harold Wilson and delivered by Queen Elizabeth II at the state opening of parliament in the House of Lords." The story continued: "Queen Elizabeth rode to the House of Lords, where she read the speech from a gilded throne, in a glass coach drawn by six horses" (the image is a bit blurred, but it was on the teley).

Speeches, speeches! Texts, texts! Problems, problems! Maybe the machine can save us. I am told there is a man at UCLA who has a machine which can compare 999 texts at one instant, and with a slight adjustment, 9,999. What the machine could do in reconstructing Bede's homilies, I do not know. In the London *Public Advertiser*

---

[55] David Laing (ed.), *The Works of John Knox* (Edinburgh, 1864), VI, 227-273.
[56] "Ghost Writing and History," XX (Autumn 1953), 460.
[57] Nov. 4, 1964, p. 5.

at various times 1769-1772, there appeared the *Letters of Junius,* which, when collected, ran to three volumes (although called *letters* they have been traditionally classified as *orations*). Who wrote them? Ah, that is the mystery. Various scholars have tried various means of identifying the author. The traditional view is that they were written by Sir Philip Francis—this has been the view since 1812. Two years ago Alvar Ellegård put the machine to work on the problem of authorship. Using samples of writing done by possible suspects, he had digital computers process 1,604,800 word samples. The machines did not stutter a moment. They came up with the answer, Sir Philip Francis.[58]

Finally, may I say that although I see various persons taking notes, there are no visible signs of my remarks being recorded on disc or tape. So if I have said something which may haunt me, I will have to reply when confronted, "What is your text?"[59]

---

[58] Alvar Ellegård, *Who Was Junius?* (Stockholm, 1962).

[59] As a concluding citation, two appeals for accuracy in reporting speech texts might be noted. Both are letters to the editor, *QJS:* George V. Bohman and J. Jeffery Auer, "To Future Editors of Collections of Speeches," XXVI (April 1940), 317-319; Wil A. Linkugel, "Oral Texts," XLVIII (December 1962), 425-427.

THE RELEVANCE OF ANCIENT LITERATURE: RECAPITULATION AND COMMENT

Roger A. Hornsby

My presence before you bears witness to the power of rhetoric, of the forms of persuasion, of the art of appealing to the emotions. Now I see the full import of the seemingly simple request to recapitulate this conference, and too late I realize how rash I was to accede to that request. Ancient literature warned me of sirens, but, nevertheless, I ignored those *exempla* and rushed to my folly. For I, who am neither a poet nor a rhetor, but only a classicist, come before you, dazzled by the talks I have heard. They, each in turn, have been impressive and persuasive, so that they leave me speechless. And so I shall not attempt to use any of the arts of rhetoric in my few remarks, for I realize now how little I know of such matters. But instead I shall speak as simply as I can, recapitulating and commenting as truthfully as possible.

Briefly, then, I shall review the wealth which the conference has laid before us. Mr. Black defined and discussed enthymematic and exhortative and their frames of reference as two genres of rhetorical discourse. He then went on to relate these two genres of rhetoric to the comedic and the mythic, pointing out in the one the moral judgment of laughter and how men's lives are changed by the other. In so doing he drew to our attention the relevance of "the typological approach of literary criticism to rhetoric" and "rhetoric's angle of vision" to literature.

Mr. Brockett suggested the possible approaches criticism can take to a work of art and the presuppositions about literature which underlie those approaches. Of these he discussed specifically instrumental criticism, for in the conception of poetry as instrument for affecting audiences he discovers that poetry and rhetoric most clearly overlap, and furthermore, ever one to aid the underdog, he finds it the approach commanding least esteem today. Judiciously surveying instrumental criticism, he concluded that while it asks worthwhile questions it unsatisfactorily answers them.

Mr. Herrick attacked the problem of the beginnings of prose tragedy, demonstrating that the Italian critics of the sixteenth century condemned the early specimens of so misguided a genre; that it began again, fumblingly, in English two centuries later, and that Ibsen eventually established it in the nineteenth century.

At the opening of the second session Mr. Weinberg discussed formal analysis as the art of discovering the internal organization of a work and argued that such analysis is relevant to philosophical treatises, rhetorical compositions, and poetic genres. Such analyses involve evaluation of the particular work. He then argued that rhetorical composition depended for its form on the audience for which it was intended, unlike, on the one hand, philosophical treatises in which the audience is entirely absent and on the other hand, poetry, in which the audience is both entirely absent and entirely present. To illustrate these theoretical distinctions Mr. Weinberg, admitting that the analyst must at times wonder whether he has a poetical or a rhetorical or a mixed work before him, analyzed *Madame Bovary* as a poetic work and *Candide* as a rhetorical work.

Mr. Krieger argued the position of contextualism, which defines rhetoric as the use of the available means of persuasion concerning a propositional claim that can be referred to independently of the discourse. It is related to decision and action. Poetry, however, is not this, for it is related to contemplation and the free play that accompanies it—the contemplation that frees words from their normal semantic and syntactic limitations and that frees our existential world from the contingencies within which our will-driven propensities for action restrict it. Contextualism, while it may downgrade poems usually accepted as poetry, i.e., the allegorical, the satirical, the didactic, does open "our awareness to the other than rhetorical dimensions in a poem which we might otherwise think of as mainly rhetorical—dimensions that can convert it into . . . something rhetorical analysis might never lead us to discover." The *persona* has been a major device that contextualist critics have used to effect this conversion. Mr. Krieger analyzed Pope's *Epistle to Dr. Arbuthnot* in these terms, showing how the P. of Pope's poem is just such a *persona* and how the rhetorical analysis of Elder Olson falls short of "explaining the poem."

Mr. Murphy this morning remarked wittily on the problems, importance, and significance of getting a fair copy of a speech, discovering what sort of copy it is, and of the kind of attention and appreciation which should be given to various sorts of texts.

Mr. Bryant, concluding the formal presentation of papers, observed what literary scholars today seem to have in mind when they include rhetoric in their vocabulary. His purview ranged from rhetoric as formal techniques codified in books called rhetorics, to rhetoric as a phase of the theory of poetry, the use of the concept of rhetoric as explicit recognition of the relations between audience and works. Mr. Bryant argued further that much literature, "though first of all a hypothetical verbal structure existing for its own sake," characteristically encompasses ethical, political, or public events and the instruments and dynamics which affect those events. A total criticism, then, will include rhetorical criticism.

If I have in this brief recapitulation of the papers traduced any speaker's argument, falsified, or brutally mutilated it, I can only plead the press of time, not willful maliciousness.

Conferences never give us world enough and time. Indeed, at this conference too, one of the recurrent motifs has been the theme of time pressing. The press of time often pressed arguments to extreme statements which in turn repeatedly forced apologies from the speakers for schematizing that which ought not to be so sharply outlined. But such are the conditions of our lives.

Several other themes have also been evident in the conference: the concern over the significance of the audience for testing and evaluating a work, the need for specificity in arguments, the sense of frustration at not being able to develop a theory which embraces a "total criticism," the suspicion that Aristotle and his handbooks are somewhat less than the *sine qua non* for a discussion of rhetoric and poetics. But above all has been the concern for defining the two topics which are presumably the chief business of the conference: rhetoric and poetic. The terms have been either left undefined or defined in a variety of ways, but no agreement has been reached on what is meant by rhetoric or poetic. Mr. Brockett properly suggested that this would be in the nature of things, for none of the participants have agreed upon basic assumptions. Mr. Hartman's question of last evening made this point eminently clear, as did Mr. Bryant's paper this morning. Criticism is, as the reasonable voice of Mr. Brockett informed us yesterday, a rhetorical venture. Each paper has indeed been an essay which has sought to gain our acquiescence. In a world as alienated as ours is, is it any wonder that common agreement is so elusive a thing?

To a classicist the whole conference has been fascinating, for rhetoric is the backbone of ancient literature, but possibly not rhetoric as it seems to me it has often been understood at this conference. When I was a schoolboy beginning the study of Latin, I had to learn, among other things, the rhetorical figures: synecdoche, alliteration, homoeteleuton, oxymoron, hysteron proteron, and all the rest which are found in any good Latin or Greek grammar. I was expected to be able to define these figures and note them whenever I came across them in a passage of prose or poetry. These struck me at the time as yet more useless bits of information that I was forever being tested on, for never was it made clear what function these figures served, beyond being ornamental devices which the ancient writers for reasons known only to them employed. They were like plums in a pudding, and rather dismal plums at that—or so it seemed to me at the time. The figures appeared to be used indiscriminately and purposelessly. I failed to see why they could not be removed, for they seemed to make no difference to the text and their removal would have made my life simpler. Neither teacher in school or college, nor handbook ever saw fit to illuminate me about the function of figures in literature. The attitude of such teachers and handbooks comes, I have since discovered, from the Renaissance and a rather naive understanding of form. Renaissance scholars, as Mr. Herrick showed yesterday, could often be misguided by their mechanical application of precept and injunction in their fancied following of the ancients. Significantly, I might note, no major writer indebted to the classics, such as Dante or Shakespeare, seems to have fallen into such scholarly nonsense. The naive attitude about form, an attitude which began in the Renaissance, accounts, I suspect, in large measure for the pejorative connotation rhetoric enjoys today. However, in my own education I discovered upon carefully reading Plato and specifically the dialogues of the first tetralogy, the *Euthyphro, Apology, Crito* and *Phaedo*, that Socrates was using rhetoric, its principles of organization as well as its figures, and nowhere more so than in his *Apology* where he specifically disclaims any connection with the forms of persuasion. From that discovery, it was a short step to the realization that Plato in all of these dialogues used rhetoric to inform his work, to give it its significance, to render it organic, for the meaning of a Platonic dialogue—as philosophical a treatise as ever was—uniquely occurs in "these words in this order," to quote Mr. Krieger in his comment on defining poetry, and for the first tetralogy "in these works in this order," we might amend. The "action," if you will, of a Platonic dialogue is as carefully worked out as that of any Greek drama. Consider the arrangement of point of view in such a dialogue as the *Symposium*, wherein we witness the dialogue refracted through four sets of "eyes," or consider how artful Plato is in the *Phaedo* in the placing of the scene. Surely the famous last line of that dialogue is justified only by the arrangement, the organization, of all which precedes it, not only in the *Phaedo* but in the other three dialogues of the tetralogy as well. The effectiveness of that last line is comparable to the success of the last line in Keat's *Ode on a Grecian Urn*. I have never seen published a rhetorical analysis or indeed a "poetic" analysis of these works of Plato, though it is becoming clearer to classicists that Plato's dialogues can only be understood fully in the light of such considerations.

Poetic and rhetoric are integral in ancient literature. We might almost say rhetoric is for ancient literature the means of forming the work, or informing it, as Allen Tate says. Plot, even plot as it was defined by Aristotle in the *Poetics*, when one examines the drama of ancient Greece, is a kind of rhetorical term.

But it was not Plato only who used rhetoric to inform his work. Homer too did so. After all, the organization of the *Iliad* is based on and informed by that well-known rhetorical figure hysteron proteron. The *Iliad* is a gigantic chiasmus or ring composition. Even the notion which we heard about last night—the *persona*—is a common rhetorical principle in ancient poetry. Poets such as Hesiod and Pindar as well as Horace constantly use it. The poet assumes a *persona* in his poems to mark him off clearly from the historical person. All this is done consciously and deliberately, and is the functional means whereby the poem is changed from "mere" rhetoric to "poetry." In his epinician odes—those occasional poems which superficially appear to be as "nonpoetic" as Mr. Weinberg thinks *Candide* is—Pindar through his mask transcends the occasional aspect of the poems and makes them lyrics whose significance is valid for all readers. The *persona* is the basis for the most passionate lyrics of Catullus. The missing of this point of the *persona* has obscured for a long time the achievement of Catullus as a lyric poet, and for a hundred years or so this failure has sidetracked, especially in the English-speaking world, the criticism of Catullus into profitless thickets of biography and history. Of course the grandest *persona* of all is Socrates, though of a different sort from these I have mentioned. Horace too, like the rest of the ancient writers, used rhetoric to inform his odes, not only the great Roman odes of book III, but also those seemingly unrhetorical ones which concern love or passion.

To understand the rhetoric of a work, the rhetorical arrangement, it has been sometimes suggested, is to gain an added dimension to the work. This seems to me false. Rather, rhetoric is not an added dimension, it is the means of organizing the work; it is the basis for understanding, comprehending the work; it is the basis for the "poetics" of the work. It is the means the author used to create his work and it is also the means whereby he wants us to understand it. The ancient notion of *docere et delectare* is not a trivial one, nor so mean a one as the English translation suggests. *Docere* means fundamentally to know, to show, as well as to tell, to inform. The failure to give the full connotative value to this word has reduced that noble phrase to a cliché which falsifies the ancient world and its perception. The English translation suggests propaganda and sentimentality. But if we reflect only a moment we will be aware that the ancients were as bored as we are by propaganda and sentimentality. Witness the way Catullus or Petronius or even Cicero handles poetasters. But the ancient writers never made the peculiar modern assumption that a work exists in some sort of vacuum, that it does not have an audience. No poet, philosopher, or prose writer ever thought he worked solely for himself. They were concerned that others should know and understand, for they knew that to know was to be delighted. Aristotle, after all, tells us at the opening of the *Metaphysics* that all men thrill to know (oregontai). The Greek verb suggests the close connection between physical passion and the desire for knowledge, a notion common in Greek literature in, for example, Plato's works where the language of love is used often to describe the imparting as well as the apprehending of knowledge. One need only consider the extended metaphor of love in the *Symposium* or the *Phaedrus* as the means to knowledge.

These remarks lead us then to the notion that ancient writers were concerned with the moral aspects of a work of art. There was no divorce between art and morality such as is so fashionable to demand today. But by morality I mean something comparable to what Mr. Black discussed yesterday as "frame of reference." Indeed Mr. Black's comments on frame of reference would have won the agreement of Plato. Both Aristotle and Plato are agreed that art has a moral concern; where they differ is in the sort of man who can produce art. For Plato only a man who knows the truth, who knows the 'Idea of the Good' can create a true work of art. For Aristotle, on the other hand, the author's personal morality is not of great interest in the consideration of a work of art. Only the moral integrity of the work concerns Aristotle. A man who might be a child-beater in private could, conceivably, create an intensely moral work. Even laughter as a means of moral judgment is not un-Greek, for the Aristophanic comedies surely demonstrate it. To try to keep art separate from the moral concerns of the world, to keep poetry distinct from truth, would have been regarded as a most odd notion by ancient writers. That famous love affair of Dido and Aeneas succeeds as literature and art because of its very fidelity to truth. Dido dies in a manner not unlike Emma Bovary. Both women, note, have already done the fatal deed but are not yet dead: Dido stabs herself, Emma drinks her poison in a final romantic and self-deluded enthusiasm, and then both learn the truth of themselves. Only at the moment of death do they perceive the bankruptcy of their lives.

In all these notions I have been discussing about ancient literature it is apparent that rhetoric and poetics are intertwined and inextricable. Rhetoric and poetics begin not with Aristotle but with Homer, and there is no distinction between the two in Homer, in the Greek lyric poets, or the Greek dramatists. Even in Isocrates we read that what distinguishes prose from poetry is metrics, not rhetoric or poetics. It is true that the development of a technē in the ancient world had a long history. But these technai were paedagogic tools, useful for organizing a particular piece of work. The Platonic objection to them came about because the Sophists tried to pretend that the technai were other than what they are. Aristotle was not primarily concerned with this problem. His handbooks are just that, handbooks, useful but limited works. He separates rhetoric and poetics to discuss drama and speech writing, but he knew, he must have known, that the two are intimately joined. His illustration of enthymeme, for example, comes from Euripides' *Medea*. Aristotle's handbooks are not bibles, despite what some would have us believe. To rely on handbooks of any sort, even Aristotle's, only leads us astray and creates the illusion that we know when we do not. The mechanical and arbitrary use of them leads to false knowledge. Only by studying what the actual works of art do can we come to any serious understanding of art, or to put it another way, of any form of discourse. This very point has been implicit in many of the remarks made by the speakers at this conference, not least of whom have been Mr. Black, Mr. Krieger, and Mr. Bryant.

From these observations it is clear, I imagine, that I too believe rhetoric and poetics make a false dichotomy, that art has connections with the world of men, and that it is moral. Rhetoric is not, it seems to me, what the Sophists did, though what they did do has been a vexed problem since the bias against the Sophists has been so strong because of Plato, as Mr. Bryant brought out this morning. This point was alluded to in the discussion periods at several sessions and came into prominence this morning when Mr. Herrick commented on the lack of vocabulary for poetics except for the terms "plot," "character," "thought," and "diction," in modern critical thinking and the consequent borrowing of terms from rhetoric. It would seem that one could take this observation a step further and suggest that even as for the ancients so for the moderns, the very lack of vocabulary might argue for the essential unity of poetics and rhetoric. (I should perhaps add that I found this morning's discussion one of the most fruitful of all, for the conferees' basic difference came sharply clear in the discussion of language and object.)

This brings me to one other topic which has been touched on and canvassed in part in this conference. That is criticism and the problem of evidence. Criticism is chiefly concerned, I should imagine we would agree, with the illumination of the text, of the genre, and even perhaps of a whole period in literary history. The kinds of criticism and its modes of attack are as varied as Mr. Brockett outlined yesterday. But withall it is just this point which makes the business so fascinating. We should argue about what we are doing, for criticism by its very nature feeds on itself; it is as Northrup Frye has recently said, a phoenix-like creature which dies only to be reborn in each new attack. If there were not areas of disagreement, we would very likely never discover what or why we do what we do. We would never discover, very likely, what evidence is pertinent, for as in any such inquiry we can see what evidence is pertinent only after it has been shown to be so. We would, in short, never learn to ask the right questions in the right order. As Mr. Brockett suggested this morning we probably will never attain a complete criticism, but our object all sublime is no doubt to keep on trying.

Dean Stuit in opening the conference noted the significance and value of interdisciplinary conferences such as this one. For me and for several of my colleagues in the Classics Department, such has been the case. But now I shall end these remarks by pointing out that the conference itself has been, when one thinks about it, an excellent example of that most pervasive of all rhetorical figures in ancient literature and even in modern, the ring-composition. I am pleased Mr. Bryant invited me to close the circle.

THE PARTICIPANTS

Edwin Black is Associate Professor of Speech and Theatre Arts at the University of Pittsburgh. He has published various articles on rhetorical subjects, and his *Rhetorical Criticism: a Study in Method* (1965) was in press at the time of the conference.

Oscar G. Brockett, Professor of Speech and Theatre at Indiana University, is a former editor of the *Educational Theatre Journal.* His special fields are dramatic theory and criticism and European theatre history. He is author of *The Theatre: an Introduction* (1964).

Donald C. Bryant is Professor of Speech at The University of Iowa and is a former editor of the *Quarterly Journal of Speech.* In rhetoric and criticism his publications include "Rhetoric: Its Function and Its Scope" (*QJS*, December 1953). He has written also on Edmund Burke and eighteenth-century parliamentary speakers.

Marvin T. Herrick is Professor of English at the University of Illinois. Among his many publications relating to rhetoric, poetic, and drama of the Renaissance are *Comic Theory in the Sixteenth Century* (1950), *Tragicomedy: its Origin and Development in Italy, France, and England* (1955), and *Italian Tragedy in the Renaissance* (1965).

Roger Hornsby, Associate Professor of Classics at The University of Iowa, has published various articles on Plato, Greek drama, and Latin poetry. His book on *Understanding Latin Poetry* is currently being considered for publication.

Murray Krieger, Carpenter Professor of Literary Criticism at The University of Iowa, is one of the leading "contextualist" critics. His recent publications include *The Tragic Vision* (1960) and *A Window to Criticism: Shakespeare's Sonnets and Modern Poetics* (1964).

Richard Murphy, a former editor of the *Quarterly Journal of Speech,* is Professor of Speech at the University of Illinois. He has published many articles on public address, including "The Speech as Literary Genre" (*QJS*, April 1958), and is co-editor of Joseph Priestley's *Lectures on Oratory and Criticism* (1965).

Bernard Weinberg, a distinguished critic and historian of criticism, is Chairman of the Department of Romance Languages at the University of Chicago. His exhaustive *History of Literary Criticism in the Italian Renaissance* in two volumes appeared in 1961. More recently he has published *The Art of Jean Racine* (1963).

[96]

33-101